Praise for

On the Breath of Song

When you take this book into your hands, you may reasonably expect to learn how to form (or join) a choir that sings to the dying and their loved ones. You are in for a surprise. Just as the experience of hospice singing turns out to be about much more than offering soothing bedside song, Kathy Leo's clear guidance for a hospice choir turns out to be the very least of what this delicious book delivers. *On the Breath of Song* embodies what it means to be really alive, wherever a person may currently be along the spectrum from birth to dying. It's about what it is to be truly present with this moment, whatever it may hold. Kathy's stories of singing to the dying remind us of our rich and complicated humanity, how every human life brims with love and loss. Her words put us in touch with our imperfection and with the ever-present possibility of opening beyond what we supposed could be. She helps readers to step through the door into the room where our own deaths (and those of our loved ones) will one day occur, and to be able to rest in that realization. Revelations abound. Kathy Leo is endowed with an uncommonly tender heart and a well of wisdom filled by years of experience. On top of that, she can write.

— Jan Frazier, spiritual and writing teacher. Author of
When Fear Falls Away, The Freedom of Being, Opening the Door
and *The Great Sweetening*

on the breath of Song

the practice of bedside singing for the dying

KATHY LEO

COPYRIGHT © 2016 KATHY LEO

All rights reserved. No part of this publication may be reproduced, distributed, or transmitted in any form or by any means, including photocopying, recording, or other electronic or mechanical methods, without the prior written permission of the publisher, except in the case of brief quotations embodied in critical reviews and certain other noncommercial uses permitted by copyright law. For permission requests, contact the author at the address below.

Printed in the United States of America. First Edition.

Contact and Ordering Information:
Send questions and comments to
Kathy Leo/Hallowell www.hallowell-singers.org
To order copies of this book go to
www.BreathofSong.com

ISBN 978-0-9969719-4-2

To order Hallowell CDs "Angels Hovering Round" and "Love Call Me Home" go to: www.hallowell-singers.org. For more hospice related music visit these sites:
www.amidonmusic.com
https://marycaybrass.com/

Cover Art by Roderick MacIver (herondance.org)
Book and cover design by the Booksmyth, Ginger Cat Designs, Shelburne Falls, MA wwwthebooksmythpress@gmail.com

Poem, "You Who Let Yourselves Feel: Enter the Breathing" is from "Part One, Sonnet IV", *Sonnets to Orpheus, by Rainer Maria Rilke.* Taken from *In Praise of Mortality: Selections from Rainer Maria Rilke's Duino Elegies and Sonnets to Orpheus,* translated from German and edited by Anita Barrows and Joanna Macy. © Riverhead, 2005.

For Dinah Breunig

And for all of those who are no longer among us, who invited us to sing around them as they died and to the families and loved ones who miss them.

Contents

13   INTRODUCTION
        STORIES
        When the Words Won't Come
        Guidance
        Dinah, My Teacher

27   I: THE PRACTICE OF SINGING FOR THE DYING
29   PRACTICE
33   PREPARATION
        STORIES
        Becoming a Small and Quiet Presence;
        Holding Each Other Up

45   II: INSIDE THE SACRED SPACE OF THE DYING
47   APPROACHING
        STORIES
        A Moment With Eileen

53   STANDING CLOSE TO DEATH
        STORIES
        You Have All You Need
        Rising Into the Stars

59   CHANGE
        STORIES
        Epiphany
        A Gesture

66   GATHERING
        STORIES
        Love Around You
        Thanksgiving
        The Real Funeral

75 THE SHAPE OF FAMILY
    STORIES
    To Die at Home
    Forgiveness Brings Light
    A Social Visit With Martha and Leo
    When Does the Singing Come?
    Children at the Bedside
    Singers Keeping Company

100 TEACHERS AND FURTHER STORIES
    STORIES
    The World Grows Quiet
    Devotion
    Equanimity

124 THE SONGS WE SING
    STORIES
    Our Songs Grow Wings
    Beyond the Book—Two Stories
    Thuma Mina

137 WHAT IF . . .
    STORIES
    Right On Time

140 EMOTIONS
    STORIES
    Is This O.K.?

144 A PLACE FOR GRIEF TO REST
    STORIES
    Grief Beyond Words
    Becoming Almost Invisible

155 INTEGRATION/CREATING CLOSURE/PROCESSING AFTER A SING
    STORIES
    Outside in Circle
    When the Tears Come

165   III: COMMUNITY
167   THE COMMUNITY AND HEALTH OF HALLOWELL
                  STORIES
                  Source of Sound and Spirit
                  Wellness
                  Accepting and Integrating New Members

177   IV: PERSONAL REFLECTIONS
179   WHAT DRAWS ONE TO BE WITH THE DYING
                  STORIES
                  Edges
                  Life, Death, Walk
                  What We Bring Home

191   V: OTHER VOICES
                  SINGERS' VOICES
                  CALL AND RESPONSE

221   VI: BASIC GUIDELINES
                  GUIDELINES FOR THE PRACTICE OF
                  BEDSIDE SINGING FOR THE DYING

233   ACKNOWLEDGMENTS

on the breath of song

INTRODUCTION

Photo: John Nopper

Dinah Breunig lay resting in her husband's arms, surrounded by family and friends from church and community, while we filled her tiny bedroom with songs. As she drew her final breaths in this world, Hallowell took our first breaths. Dinah's generous spirit, and the family's invitation for others to be with her during her dying, to sing around her bedside in joy and reverence, is the reason we are now able to offer this gift to anyone in our community who desires to leave this world on the breath of song.

How does this practice of bedside singing take shape? What is at its heart? Knowing the songs well, rehearsing, building repertoire and creating a connection between the singers are all necessary and essential as is learning how to sing in small groups, to blend voices, to be strong on a part in four part harmony. But there is more beyond the singing.

A death room is as changeable and lyrical as the chords and harmonies we sing. When we cross the threshold into a room where a family is gathered around their loved one's bed, we enter a holy space, a sanctuary, a place where we are close to the truth of our living. We become open channels for whatever lies in wait. We leave our expectations and hopes outside with our egos. It is in this state of grace that we are most receptive, most able to learn what is before us and to respond to the energy in an openhearted way. The songs we choose, the way we relate to the person in the bed or those surrounding it, how long we stay or how softly or loudly we sing, where we stand, whether or not we touch or remain distant, all of this comes to us if we enter the room, each time, as if it were our first sing.

There are common, practical questions that arise when a new group is unfolding. How do I relate to my personal grief while singing at a deathbed? How do we know what to sing? How long to stay? Should I touch the person in the bed? How do I relate to the family? How do we prepare for a sing or process afterward? What can we expect as hospice singers? My hope for this guide book is to answer these questions in a practical matter-of-fact way while communicating an understanding that there is a place "beyond the rules." There exists a deeper landscape. This is a practice of compassion and witnessing, of being fully present in a place where the heart opens, and where the unexpected occurs. It is a practice of acceptance of what-is.

This book holds stories of those who have invited us to their bedside, allowed us to stand beside them and sing to their process of dying. Many souls have been our teachers. May their stories bring you close to the experience of what it is to make choices at the end of life that support the possibility of a more conscious death. May you feel, through these stories, the way music can find a place among the last breaths of a dying person and become part of the mystery of death.

Over the past years, we have traveled throughout the country to teach workshops that have helped launch other hospice choirs in different communities. Each community has its own strengths, needs and unique personality, and shapes its choir to meet these differences. Some choirs are formed from hospice volunteers who work hard to build a repertoire and learn music by having weekly rehearsals. Others are formed from an already existing choir with a desire and willingness to use music as a therapeutic offering at the end of life. Many are a combination of both of these.

However a community creates a group, we share the same intention of service. We receive as much as we give. The love we exchange is authentic and genuine and translates into every aspect of our living. It reaches into the world to make those gentle and barely noticeable heart changes that affect each one of us. Each visit we make invites change in cultural beliefs around how we care for our loved ones at the end of life. Bedside singing invites us to stand close to, rather than distant from, death. It is a blessing to those of us fortunate and privileged enough to be welcomed into the lives of the dying.

Use this guide book however it may serve you; to answer questions as you are forming a new group, to offer support as your group evolves, to inspire you and give you courage and confidence to bring beautiful harmony to the bedsides of the dying, or to explore your personal relationship with death and therefore with the joy of living in the world until we pass on to whatever may be next.

Stories

❧

When the Words Won't Come

When I visit my mom, now in her eighties, and it's time to say good-bye after a short visit that often feels long, bags all packed, bedding washed and put away, we say our ritual good-byes. We hug and kiss and say thank you for this and that and then suddenly, in our moment of leaving, it seems the entire time of our visit takes a whole shape. No matter what we did, said or didn't say, the time we spent becomes sacred. Saying goodbye fills itself with emotion and questions. When will we see each other again? And the unspoken question--the one we all think but don't say as her health continues to decline--will we see each other again. She walks to the door with us and stands watching and waving as we drive away. She has always done this--walking as far as she can, holding us with her eyes until we are out of sight. Who knows how long afterward she stands looking into the empty space where we just were.

I have done this with my own children when they come in and out of my life. Saying goodbye never fails to bring a lump to my throat that holds back the swell of tears that want to come so that what I might want to say remains unspoken. It does get said though, just not in words, when I follow them out to their car or walk to the end of the driveway, wave and watch the car disappear down the dirt road and when I stand in the silence and watch the dust settle.

When a loved one is dying, and the final goodbye is hovering in the air, on the breath, poised in the heart, on the tongue, sometimes the words get caught. Sounds won't seem to shape themselves into words. Sometimes something else wants to be said; a thought, a memory, an intention, the feeling of loss or despair, grief or love. Sometimes we find another way to speak; a hand held, lips on skin, a touch on the top of the head, a tender way of looking, a small vase of flowers, moistening of dry lips, a song, a circle of strangers with kind hearts singing around the bed. Songs can say things that are hard to speak, soften the air, and clear a space for a different kind of language to be spoken.

When Hallowell is invited to sing at the bedside of a dying person, we do our very best to arrive with clear minds and hearts, in a state of readiness to be present and to listen deeply for what we might offer through music. We feel our way around the room with eyes and senses open. We wait for guidance to come. We are aware of emotion, relationships, the level of grief, and, most of all, love. Over and over we say, "I love you," "I will miss you," "I want to help you to die." We say it through the words of songs we choose; *"How deeply I'm connected to your soul."* We say, I'm here, by singing, *"I, my loving vigil keeping."* We say, you are not alone, *"friends carry me over, love call me home."* We give hope in song when we sing, *"There'll be no sorrow there."*

There are messages we can speak through the lyrics of songs we choose. Sometimes, we choose songs in other languages or we simply hum around the bed, another way to say what words can't. When the words won't come, maybe the songs will say what wants to be spoken. The sounds or the poetry of music can speak to the soul leaving or the ones staying. Perhaps the songs can speak for the one dying or the ones saying goodbye.

When our songs are still lingering in the ear and the heart, in the air in the room, maybe then, when the family looks into the space we had just filled, with their hearts a bit more broken open, maybe that's when the tongue will find the words to speak what is still left unsaid.

Guidance

We are singing on the sidewalk in downtown Brattleboro, outside of the River Garden where the Wake Up To Dying event has been ongoing for the past two days. People have come for workshops to share and hear stories about death and dying, to explore spiritual questions and thoughts, to write on the blackboard, "Before I die, I want to_____" "Write a book, fall in love, win a grammy, see my son, dance on stage, smoke legalized weed, have a grandchild, accept death."

Twelve of us have come on this Saturday evening to sing as a way to support this project that offers a safe space for conversation and dialogue about death. We choose a place against the building so we can hear each other. Although we consider ourselves bedside singers, and being at the bedside always remains at the heart of our intention, you might see us on the street from time to time or opening for a concert that benefits our local Brattleboro Hospice.

Or you might hear us as a full group singing in a church that has to close its doors after hundreds of years due to a lack of funding and a shrinking congregation. We invite those gathered to remain silent and be anointed by the sounds. We are singing to their grief and loss.

Every year we sing for the Memorial Garden Planting ceremony that Brattleboro Hospice organizes as a place for those who have lost a loved one to come, to plant something, to be in circle and hear poems and names read and our songs sung.

This evening, we are street singers calling people to come and experience Wake Up to Dying. There are not many people out in town this evening. We sing "By the Waters of Babylon" in four parts. We sing "No One Stands Alone." *Hold my hand, all the way, every hour, every day, from here to the great unknown. Take my hand, let me stand, where no one stands alone.*

Shop doors start to open. Walkers stop to listen. And then Lauren comes walking towards us. She beams at us and opens her arms. I pull her into an embrace, tuck her into the soprano section beside me, and she joins easily and seamlessly in the singing of "I Still Have Joy."

Lauren was a junior in high school when her mother, Dinah, died. She was as engaged as any bright and lively teenager would be at that time, acting in a play, singing, dancing, socializing. And yet, Lauren was fully aware that her mother's life force was waning and that she would die soon. She and her father, Fred, were with Dinah when she took her last breath.

I met Lauren and her sister Katharine in 2002, when I became Dinah's hospice volunteer. Katharine is the older sister, then nineteen years old. She has Down syndrome and was always home when I would come to spend some evening time with Dinah while Fred went out to a church meeting.

The family welcomed friends into their home to witness the way death could be possible, in the arms of family, comfortable and tended with love in a safe and familiar place. Dinah has been our guiding star these many years as we continue to sing for hundreds of families in our community.

It should not surprise me then, that twelve years after her death, her daughter Lauren would come strolling into our circle just in time to sing "I Still Have Joy." "I'm only in town for 24 hours," Lauren says, shaking her head and grinning. As she walks away, I look to the clouds and whisper "Thanks" to Dinah. Again.

The following is a piece I wrote for Dinah Breunig before Hallowell was formed.

Dinah, My Teacher

I'm not sure exactly when I started to love Dinah as a dear friend and teacher. Maybe it was the snowy night we drove together to hear her husband Fred's holiday concert in Dublin, New Hampshire. As I navigated my way through slippery winter roads, Katharine chattered happily to us from the back seat saying things like "I love my life," making us both gasp and look at each other in wonder. Later, I watched Dinah adoring Fred from where she sat in a soft arm chair placed among the hard church pews, brought in for her comfort, her portable oxygen tank in a small shoulder bag on the floor beside her. She was a queen that night, happy to be out in the world among friends, hearing the joyful music her husband was singing, her daughter exuberant beside her.

Or maybe I started to love her on that quiet night at home when Katharine, Dinah, and I snuggled on the couch while I read aloud from the book Dinah was too breathless to read to Katharine.

Maybe still, it was one of those evenings I helped her with the king sized quilt she was making for her brother's wedding gift. I was with her when she finished it. I helped her feed yards of fabric through her sewing machine, watched as she reinforced stitches and guided the last edges carefully through. Together we pressed the final seams, cut loose threads, trimmed and perfected the pieces of fabric she had so patiently transformed into a quilt. We laid the finished quilt out on Katharine's bed. Dinah sat down to catch her breath and then to take it in, to look over this work of art and love she had brought to completion in her last days. She cried. Katharine and I exclaimed at its beauty. I admired its perfection. The dark stars floated among lilacs and bluets, every point touching the next seam exactly as it should.

Once, as I watched Dinah work, helping her with lifting, folding, and fetching, I told her I knew I was in the presence of a master. Her work was so careful and meticulous. What might it feel like to work that carefully, I wondered. At home, I worked on my own quilt, one I was making for my mother's 70th birthday from scraps of my grandmother's clothes I had taken after Grandma died the previous February. My sewing room was littered with scraps, threads and flannels of blues and purples. My quilt was growing out of a center angel made from Grandma's skirt as well as silks and velvets. The measuring was careless. The corners didn't exactly match up. Still, it held its own beauty. I told Dinah I would never show her mine and we laughed because we knew our differences were perfect. She said she was the technician and I was the artist. You, I told her, are the teacher, and I am the student.

One year ago on my birthday, I began my hospice training. Now Dinah is living her final hours, taking her last counted breaths. She has been my first hospice patient. And it has been a wonderful, sad, unexpected blessing to be Dinah's student and friend. For over seven months, I have visited this family once a week. In the fall, I froze tomatoes from their garden. I fixed soups and stir fries, fried potatoes, and made puddings. I washed up the dishes, swept the floors. Every week I would clean off the stairs, sweep them one by one, wash each step clean with a damp cloth, so that at night, when Dinah made her way to bed, she could rest on a clean step to catch her breath and not sit among the dust balls that bothered her so much. I grew to love her daughters, especially Katharine, their child with Down syndrome, who is as open and loving as we all strive to become. Lauren would often be out when I was there, busy with her active teenager's schedule, in music, sports, and theater. I would come on the evenings Fred needed to be out so Dinah wouldn't be alone.

She is alone now in her dying, the way it must be. The night Dinah finished her quilt and we laid it out in its fullness on Katharine's bed, I thought I saw something let go. I was witness to some brief moment of release, a holding on finally lifting. I noticed the physical softening of the facial muscles when something inside relaxes and accepts, the dropping of held shoulders. The next day, Fred took her with her quilt to the woman who would stitch the layers together. Then, just two days after I watched her finish it, she no longer came down the stairs, dusted or not.

On a Tuesday evening, I went to visit Dinah. Downstairs I joined a group of singers from the Guilford Community Church gathering in the small living room. Peter Amidon, music director, whispered to the singers, "We'll just go upstairs, sing one quiet song and then leave." Lise Sparrow, pastor of the church, had asked for this to happen, and everyone wants to do what Lise asks. She holds the trust of her church congregation and the community beyond in her hands like a prayer.

We found Dinah smaller already, the physical self shrinking away as the life force leaves. But when her room filled with thirty or so people, and we started to sing that "one quiet song," Dinah filled with light. We stayed for almost an hour. We sang song after familiar song, and Dinah sang along with us. When someone asked her how she was doing, she smiled and replied, "I'm as happy as a clam." The light lingered in the room for a long time after, and its glow followed each of us home.

We sang again on Thursday. People filled the small upstairs bedroom and overflowed out into the hallway. Fred sat behind Dinah, propped her up with his arms around her, and sang softly into her ear. She had a daughter on either side of her. Our voices joined to sing "By the Waters of Babylon," "Angels Hovering Round," "I Will Guide Thee" and more. Dinah drifted in and out, a look of contentment on her face. Acceptance, love, and harmony filled the room. The room was full of spirit. My dreams at night were full of spirits, guiding Dinah, showing her which way to go.

Over the next days, I made tomato lentil soup and left it in the refrigerator. I baked chocolate chip cookies. The house filled with flowers and cards, bowls and plates of food, friends and relatives, prayers and songs. There was so much love around Dinah, I think she may have been reluctant to go. Fred shared stories of her visions in the night, telling of a bountiful banquet like she had never seen before. I asked her once if her heart was at peace and she said yes and I knew that it was true. In the night, lying beside her, Fred would wake and take her hand to feel her squeeze back, rising to the surface from wherever she had been, whispering I love you to each other. He asked her if she was ready, told her it was okay to let go. Lauren, too, told her it was okay to go now.

When I saw her on her final Sunday, she didn't seem to know I was there, or that Fred's sister sat beside her quietly reading, moistening her dry lips when she needed it, keeping vigil. Dinah was already away. It was only her physical body holding on now. I kissed her lightly on the forehead as I left and told her she was surrounded by love and that everyone here had what they needed. I told her she had been a wonderful teacher and that I would miss her, and I was so blessed to have had this time with her.

I left that day, knowing I wouldn't see Dinah again in this lifetime, but I would feel her in the final stitches as I finished making my mother's quilt, more careful now after watching Dinah work, and in the songs about angels, light and beauty, and in anything that had to do with grace, life and death. Good teachers live on in their students, always.

March 11th, 2003 Dinah died last night, quietly, peacefully in her bed at home, Lauren and Fred's soft laughter floating around her as she took her final breath and let go.

The sing for Dinah was our first unofficial sing. After this experience, Noree Ennis, the patient care coordinator of Brattleboro Area Hospice at the time, had a vision. She asked me if I might create a group of singers who would visit other hospice patients. Thirty-five people answered my letter and said they would be interested. Most of those people are still singing with Hallowell today.

Twelve years later, Dinah continues to show up at the bedside with us, or on the street in downtown Brattleboro, her beautiful daughter Lauren appearing like a vision. Lauren sang with Hallowell for years until she moved across the country into the full life of a young woman. Fred is still a valued leader and a treasured tenor among us.

PART ONE

the practice of singing for the dying

Photo: John Nopper

ONE

PRACTICE

When we first started to visit the dying, to sing for people in their homes and hospital beds, we had no name for what we were doing. There were no models we knew of at the time. We learned, with the support of our local hospice staff, how best to offer our service of song with appropriate behavior for singers when going to visit people at the end of life.

At first, we referred to what we were doing as a ministry. The word ministry, however, is strongly affiliated with a religion, which we are not. We are clear that our mission in Hallowell is to be available to sing for the community, including everyone and anyone who asks for our service of song. We find songs that shape themselves to each family's beliefs, without judgement, and without the desire to impose our own values on others. As a group, we represent the differences in our greater community. We are made whole by our differences. We are Jews, Christians, Buddhists, Pagans, non-believers, deep believers, ritual-makers, those who find church in the natural world. But at the center of what shapes us as a group is the love we each have for all of humanity.

We have come to understand that what we do as bedside singers for the dying and their families is a practice. The practice includes many parts: preparing ourselves, learning how to grow quiet inside, being part of a whole, staying present while standing close to death, being nonjudgmental and respectful, knowing how to leave a sing gracefully and how to integrate what we witness. And of course, we practice our music. We learn new songs and refresh old songs. We practice blending voices in small groups, singing quietly and staying on pitch.

When we enter someone's home as Hallowell, we understand that we are being invited into a sacred space. This family has made an invitation for us, strangers, to come and stand with them in their time of transition. We come with compassion, not pity. We come to sing, not to judge. Not to change whatever is before us. We understand that death is a normal part of life and we sing to the truth and beauty that a death can bring into a family. We have learned to see the wholeness and wellness of the dying person. The concept of wellness when you are dying is not something we are taught to believe in our culture of heal, fix, change, help. Through our medical lens we are taught to make things better, that death is the ultimate failure.

One of the greatest gifts we have received through our service with Hallowell is this shift in thinking. We have been given a different lens, one that sees wholeness, wellness and health in death and dying. When the body starts to shrink away from life and a person's earth world grows smaller, there can be more room for the spirit of a being to shine through. Often, we are gifted with seeing the essence of a person, the beauty of who they truly are, the light of their souls, as they rest on their dying bed, accepting and peaceful. I don't know how many times I have heard these words from a singer during a closing circle, "He looked like an angel." Or, "She looked translucent and illuminated."

The practice asks us to show up, again and again, to stay open to learning new things about life and death and about ourselves in relationship to each other and the world. Like any practice, there will be good days and hard days. Sometimes we leave a sing with many questions. Other times we leave feeling clear, blessed and stretched in ways we did not know was possible. Each time we cross a doorway into someone else's life and witness their loss, love and grief, we have an opportunity to practice how to live our own lives with presence, humility and gratitude. This is what draws us to the bedsides of the dying. It is a great honor to be invited to such a place, so rich with life. It is a place that requires us to be alert and to experience life with our hearts and senses wide open.

In a recent workshop, a woman spoke of the difference between "normal" life and the sacred feeling of life at a bedside sing. In that moment, I realized what it is we are practicing for; when there is no difference between these places and sacred life merges with daily life. We are practicing how to remain as open and accepting anywhere in our lives; at the market, driving our car, being at a family dinner, talking with neighbors, as we are while standing in the presence of death.

TWO

PREPARATION

How do we prepare ourselves for the unknown? Each time we walk through the doorway of a stranger's home, we walk into a new territory. The inner and outer landscapes of a family's life await our open senses. We try to arrive at each sing as prepared as possible. The more awake and alert we are when we enter a space, the more receptive we will be. The better prepared we are, the more able to "read the room" and respond with grace to whatever shows up at the bedside.

Inevitably, displays of grief and emotion are expressed by the loved ones of the dying. Because we have come prepared, we are able to stay present in the face of what might otherwise be uncomfortable. When we are aware of someone's fear or pain, or we stand close to disturbing sights and smells, we keep ourselves grounded in compassion and practice acceptance. Our view of death has potential to be transformed, from something feared and ugly to something natural and beautiful.

We are as different as the days, as the songs of birds, as the passing clouds. We each find our own path to centeredness, to the state of calm we hope to be in when we arrive at a sing. Meditation, prayer, or a walk in nature are all ways to help quiet the mind.

If there is no time to ground ourselves through the practice of mindfulness or prayer before leaving for a sing, we often use the time in the car to try to enter into a state of clarity and quiet attention. We turn off the radio. Some of us ask for guidance from the universe, spirit guides, angels, God, our higher self, whoever we personally call upon when the need arises. Deep breaths or humming lubricates the vocal chords and settles the central nervous system. We might notice our thoughts. Am I making plans to visit a friend after the sing or running through a grocery list in my head? We remember that we are going to someone's bedside, to a place that will call forth all of our best qualities. It will be the only place we are. All of the chatter in our heads can rest, and we will become a prayer of song at the bedside of a dying stranger. This is an invitation to be present, to enter mystery.

On the practical side is the need to gather information about the person we are invited to visit. We find out who our person is. What does he love? Who is spending time with him as he nears the end of his life. Does she belong to a church or temple? Does she follow a religion or have a spiritual practice or community? What kind of work did this person do? Does he have a preference for a certain kind of music? Has he had a relationship with music? How old is she and what has her health journey been? All of this information informs the choices we make as we select songs. It guides us to know how to move into the space and help prepare the ground of our being so that we don't stumble as easily if the terrain becomes unfamiliar ground, rocky with unexpected emotional landscape.

An introductory initial phone call is made, if possible, as an opportunity to make a connection and to assure the family that we do not need nor expect anything from them. They do not need to prepare for our visit. They already have enough to do. We offer them the option of changing their minds about the sing at the very last minute. When I make this call, I might say to a family member, "You always have the option to cancel, even if we show up at your door. If you decide, at the last moment, that a sing is not wanted after all, you are welcome to turn us away. We understand how quickly things can change." People feel relief when this offer is made. Inviting people into a home can be an added stress for a family taking care of a loved one, no matter what the hope for the visit may be. Sometimes it is our intention alone that carries the message. And that is enough.

Just as the individual singer meets the group in as calm a state as possible, the group, as an entity, must prepare to enter someone's dying space. Gathering first to share information about who we are about to sing for, and where we are going, provides some insight, gives the group confidence, and lessens the element of surprise. A gentle reminder by the leader to grow smaller as a group is enough to change social conversation to respectful attention. When the parts are quiet, the whole is quiet. If each of us, in turn, has come prepared to be at a sing, our group will absorb this sense of slowness and move as one being into the room. Often a shared song before crossing the threshold will draw us together and unite us in mind, body and spirit.

Stories

❧

Becoming a Small and Quiet Presence, A Three-Sing Journey

We are on a three-sing journey, each family lives further south from our meeting place, so that by the last sing, we will have driven almost an hour and a half. The afternoon sun is still warm in late September. Peter drives five of us down route 9 towards Wilmington, Vermont, where we plan to meet one more alto, Sue, just done with her day of teaching in the school district where she has worked for years.

Our first sing is for Edward. His wife greets us at the door, at the top of the switchback rise of a long metal ramp, recently installed by the VA. She offers a warm embrace, as if we were long time friends, though this is our first face to face meeting. The group waits in the driveway while I enter this small country home through the front porch into the cozy living room where ruffled curtains cover dark framed windows. Plush colonial style couch and chairs face the television, where I find Edward in his recliner, feet up in resting position, oxygen tubing leading to the tank beside him. I can hear his effort to breathe as he grasps my hand and tells me how much he has always loved to sing. On the wall, I notice Jesus looking over this family. Edward's sister has come from her house just up the road. This is an old Vermont family, I have been told.

This particular group of singers is seasoned. Out of the six of us, most have been to many sings over many years. I trust them completely. I trust their level of comfort and their potential to be present and understand boundaries that create a feeling of safety for the family. On the way in the car, we talked about Edward's closeness to death, his long standing place in the community, the family business he ran for years, his religious community and church. We prepared ourselves.

And yet, when I call the group to come in, I fail to signal quieting. I do not remind them to become a small group, physically, despite the number of us. We do this by moving slowly. We do this by quieting the nervous chatter in our heads when we focus on our breath. I do not ask them to hum their way in. Edward, his wife and sister warmly welcome six singers. Sue and Edward's sister recognize each other and start to make the connection. I realize, too late, that I had forgotten, as leader, to set the tone for a quiet entrance. Our visit becomes more of a social sing. And it is a lovely social sing, respectful and yet with spaces for conversation in-between songs. We sing hymns that invite tears and stories about their church community and their faith and how it is bringing them comfort and support now. We leave with a full feeling in our hearts and make our way to the second home, where a couple and their caretaker are expecting us.

This time I remember. We gather on the walkway beside a September garden. We are surrounded by purple aster and white anenome on tall stems leaning into the path. Before I leave the group to meet Marcy and Robert, I suggest that each one take a moment to speak an intention aloud. Begin with, "May I be...."

"May I be present," says Connie, in a whisper. "May I be clear." "May I sing on pitch," Calvin replies in his bass voice, always on pitch. "May I remember to listen." "May I be guided," I say to myself as I knock on the door. "May we serve from our highest source of love." They follow me in, a few moments later, humming. Reverence flows in the door with them. The sound and feel of this sing begins in holiness. Marcy sits across the table from us, her head lists to one side, her eyes roll back in her head, her speech is garbled, the stroke having disconnected parts of her brain from her muscles. But she is fully aware of us and listens with a musician's ear to our songs. Behind us a grand piano gleams in the sunlight, scores of classical music are on the stand. Music is a source of life for this couple and we are humbled and honored when, with great effort, Marcy finds the strength to say, "beautiful," after we sing a sacred Russian Orthodox chant. We sing "Farthest Field" after Robert asks for a song about landscape and we think of the tended gardens and the way the land rolls away in sweeping meadows into the surrounding hills. *There is a land, high on a hill, where I am going. There is a voice that calls to me. Walk with me and we will see the mystery revealed. When one day we wend our way up to the farthest field.* In the silence after song, we can see Marcy attempting to speak again. Her breath changes. She moves her head slightly and opens her mouth. We are utterly still. She utters these words, clearly, "professional quality." I look over at Peter. I perceive, more than see, him sit up a bit taller and draw in his breath in gratitude. This is what he aspires to; to bring clear, pure and beautiful sound to those we sing for. Marcy bestows a blessing upon us, with great effort and beautiful grace.

By the time we find our last home for this three sing journey, darkness has descended. The family is waiting. Our timing is perfect. As a group, we move as a slow wave and approach with respectful intention. We hum our way up the wide wooden stairs. There is no need for a reminder now. We are well prepared and become the voice of benediction at the bedside.

Tina is in her early fifties. Her bewildered husband, a close neighbor, and her father, who is sitting in the back of the room in a rocker, are all with her. There is tremendous grief in this bedroom along with a sense of acceptance and equanimity in Tina. She is in her bed, wrapped in comfort; cotton pajamas, fleecy blankets and orange lamp light. She reaches for her husband's hand, pulls him closer while we sing around her. She knows what she wants. We are deeply quiet by now, each of us in our own state of inner prayerfulness after our last two sings. We sing, *"Take the gift I bring. Friends carry me over. Deep within me life is singing. Love call me home."*

We float back down the stairs on the vibrations of our hums and ease back into the darkness to form our final circle beneath the rising moon.

Holding Each Other Up

Once a month, for two hours, we gather in a bright open space, set our chairs in a circle and begin rehearsal.

Peter calls us to attention with his warm-ups. We stand up, focus, and sing up and down scales. He makes us laugh and listen. He teaches us new songs that he has carefully arranged for Hallowell. Songs that have been shared now by hundreds of others standing at bedsides around the country. Peter is a magical and particular arranger. He gives us four parts of harmony to make a whole sound, so we can be one voice, singing the feelings we want to offer. "Crossing the Bar." "I Will Guide Thee." "How Could Anyone Ever Tell You." "How Can I Keep From Singing." "I Still Have Joy." So many others.

Mary Cay brings us languages we learn to roll off of our tongues. Piles of consonants tumble out of our mouths in Serbo-Croation. African. Russian. We roll our R's and soften our T's into D's. Some of us roll our eyes. But we practice and we enfold these songs, one after another, into our hearts. And when we don't want to speak familiar words at the bedside, to pull a dying person away from the hard work they are doing, or call them back to the familiar world, we offer strange, comforting sounds in foreign languages. These songs carry a story, a feeling that resides in the words and notes. But they allow the person on their journey to continue, and possibly, to go a bit further away. Mary Cay brings us cultural bridges through the songs she gathers, so we can offer them to the dying.

We learn our songs deeply, setting them into the cells of our bodies. We don't memorize, exactly. We learn by heart. We have a By-Heart list, songs we have learned to keep, so that when we bring them to bedside, we can be present there. "Love Call Me Home," the leader will say, and we will all find it in our book. We might sing it through without ever once needing to look down at the page, but there it is, in our hands, inviting us to grab the first words of the second verse if we need to. *When the waters are cold, friends carry us over...* and the rest of the verse comes easily and naturally because it is already in our hearts. We feel the confidence that the music director instills and the security of the page before us, lest we forget our place. Whatever offers us stability and clarity at the bedside is a path to presence.

There is no final concert or performance for the bedside singer. There is no end to our rehearsal. In this way, rehearsal becomes a means unto itself. It becomes a part of the whole practice as much as any sing does.

Rehearsal tonight reminds me of the nourishing well we create when we come together to sing, share stories and process past sings. The clock says it is past the end of our time together, though in late June, there is still light in the sky. People sit, as if glued to their chairs. No one is ready to break the circle.

We have sung through the new Bach piece Calvin brought us, "Deck Thyself." We have practiced this month's By-Hearting song, "Khvalitye," a Russian orthodox chant. The room is still ringing from the gorgeous sounds of it when Joan asks to sing for a beloved friend who has just received a terminal diagnosis for leukemia. We sing "I'll Fly Away" while we offer hope for her. And then Annie reminds us of recent news, another senseless shooting. Nine black people shot to death in a church, a violent act of racial hatred that sickens us and humbles and angers us. We sing to the world of this, *"Joy Shall Come in the Morning."* Please. May it be true. Our songs become prayers.

We have already spoken of the sings we experienced this past month, people sharing impressions and pictures of the lives they witnessed and touched with these songs we know. I have spoken of Stuart and our sing for him the day before his death and the way we found him completely unresponsive to this world. Our songs fell over and around him while his son hovered in the background and his cousin sat beside him in a detached state of quiet. We remind each other how to sing to what we can't see. How to remember that hearing is the last sense to leave us when we are dying. We remember stories of near death experiences and how people in a coma may have more acute hearing and perception than we can know. We remember to believe, every time we sing, that the dying person knows we are there and can hear our singing, feel our hearts, know our intentions. We acknowledge this as a challenge and agree to rise to it each time.

Others share. The words seem to be pouring forth this evening. Maybe it's the gentle summer air. Earlier we had broken ourselves into small groups to practice among the gardens outside. Maybe it is the way one heart opening invites another to do the same. This rehearsal does not want to end. Something holds us here. Connection. Song. Love.

"Mary Alice, I say, into the thickening silence, "can you lead that one......?"

I'm gonna lift my brother up, he is not heavy.....

We sing. We stand up, move closer, hold each other in a ring.

I'm gonna lift my sister up, she is not heavy....If I don't lift her up, I will fall down.

We hold each other up. That's what we are rehearsing, I think. Just this. Nothing more.

Photo: Beth Lukin

PART TWO

inside the sacred space of the dying

Photo: John Nopper

THREE

Approaching

How do we encounter and draw close to another person, a stranger most likely, with clarity and courage? Courage being of the heart. How do we show up somewhere with our whole selves in alignment?

In our first connection with a dying person we might experience vulnerability and awkwardness, feel as if we are intruding on someone's privacy, or that we are not wanted, or don't belong. We don't know what to expect. When the person we are going to meet is nearing the end of their life, possibly in pain or feeling fear, what do we say to them? What do we have to offer and how do we find the words to begin?

When I approach a dying person, when I open the door and first step into someone else's story, I bring my smile and a quiet heart. I believe I am welcome. I have a gift to bring: the sweetness of voices in harmony to be offered around this person, a sense of calm and witness. Through the songs we are able to say, "You are not alone. We see you. We have come to be with you." I try to leave my own stories at the door before I enter; my fear or anxiety, my struggles or inadequacies. I might pause at the entrance, close my eyes, and ask spirit to be with me. And then I enter.

I believe in the wellness of the dying person. I look for the light in her eyes, if she is awake, or I look beyond to where light might be hovering around her tired body already. I believe she can hear my voice, feel my presence and perceive my emotional energy. If my heart is clear and open and my intention is good, she will know it.

I believe that hearing is not only the last sense to leave us as we die, but that our hearing becomes acute in a way we have never known before. Imagine a person is close to their final breath. They are unresponsive, perhaps in a coma or medicated into a state of seeming oblivion. Imagine while it looks this way to those of us around their bed, that person's ability to perceive has grown wings. We believe they can hear, feel and know everything we have come to offer in the way of song, comfort or love. In this way, we follow a path of kindness and offer respect for the mystery of what it means to die.

The death bed is not always a place of comfort. It can be an unsettled place. There are disturbances there, physical and emotional. The comfort must come from inside of us, from what we bring, what we believe and how we express it.

We move towards the dying person as if we come bearing good news and approach with a tender heart and with confidence that we are welcome here. We listen from the well of our ears. We quiet our thinking mind and become receptive. We are reading, gathering information, and bearing witness to this person who is no longer a stranger but has allowed us entry into his life's journey at a vulnerable time. We don't want to miss this moment because fear is trying to tell us otherwise. Though inner voices might say, "you are not doing this right," or "you don't belong here," we trust that we will know what to say or that we might not need to say anything.

When we draw close to the dying, we too are reminded that we will die. We remind ourselves to be still. Take our time. Take a person's hand. Notice the surroundings. Rest with this friend. Say the words that come naturally or just feel them and speak them through intention. All is well here. It is not ours to change. It is only a place for us to come, invited, and be.

Stories

A Moment With Eileen

I walk through the kitchen, down the narrow hall to meet Eileen resting in her bed in the living room, now turned into a bedroom, on the first floor of the house she lives in with David. The windows are open to a June breeze and white curtains move into the room with the air. Light falls across the moss colored blankets covering what is left of Eileen's shrinking body. She has not eaten well in months and hasn't had anything to eat or drink for the last few days. Her eyes are lightly closed, though I sense that she is not asleep.

I sit quietly beside her, and take in the surroundings. The bed is in the middle of the room. A couch has been moved along the wall, under the window. Chairs line the edges of the space, some piled with discarded clothes. A piano fills the far corner. Beside it, a music stand holds sheets of music. Various lotions, jars and an assortment of earrings and bracelets cover the dresser top. Lush pink peonies, cut from the garden outside the front door, spill from a glass vase. A mirror over the dresser reflects the room back to me.

For these few moments, I am alone with Eileen. When she eventually senses my presence beside her, she opens her eyes and turns to face me. Her eyes are clear pools of light. I need to ground myself, feel my feet on the floor, so as not to get lost in her gaze.

Eileen is in her mid fifties. She and David had fallen in love and gotten married just a few years after David's first wife had died of cancer. Eileen, he told me, was a gift he could not have dreamed of, bringing love and joy into his life after great loss. Once again, cancer has come to take a beloved from him. This is all too familiar to David, his wife in bed, saying goodbye to the world, saying goodbye to their love and relationship.

Eileen reaches for my hand. We sit for a moment, just looking. She knows why I am here. She has been preparing herself for the singers' visit. Although, at this fragile moment in her dying, she has no energy left to accept all of the offers for visits from friends, she has let David know that she wants what we have offered. I wait while she finds the strength to speak the words she wants to say to me. "I'm not afraid," she says. "I am so full of love." I stay with her that way for a long moment. Patient. No expectations from either of us. We are strangers and yet she has let me in. She holds me with her eyes and her fragile bony hand, and I hold on with mine.

What does love look like, I wonder, to someone who is leaving her body, this world, her life. But there it is in her eyes. It shines. It almost dances with light. And it is as easy to read as if it were written out in bold letters: **This Is Love**.

I return to the singers, where they are humming in a close circle, standing amidst the clutter of kitchen life; a sink full of dishes, open boxes of crackers on the counter, a cold pot of soup on the stove. I find my part among the vibration of notes as we ease ourselves into the room, and find places to sit and stand close to Eileen. Women have come now to fill the chairs, colorful friends from Eileen's women's group. They wear sandals and skirts, light shawls draped over bare shoulders, open faces.   David is on the couch, pale and hollow looking. His face and body language speak of sorrow, waves of grief appear as creases across his brow, around his hooded eyes.

We surround Eileen. We make music with our raw voices. Emotion flows around the room. I see heads held, handkerchiefs being pulled from pockets. This loss is anguish, fresh, raw and seemingly unbearable.   Eileen is young, a treasure among her friends. There is no way to make sense of this woman's death.

We sing, "Love Call Me Home." *Take the gift I bring, friends carry me over. Deep within me life is singing, love call me home.* Eileen opens her bright eyes and offers a blissful smile to no one in particular.

David feels miles away. Without a thought about why, I go to him, and lead him gently to Eileen's bedside while we sing. He takes my offered hand. The singers clear a path and David sits on the bed beside Eileen. Her eyes settle on him. She drinks him in and they stay that way, reaching far into each other and holding on, for the hour we sing. *May there be no sadness of farewell, when I embark.* It seems Eileen is speaking the words of our songs to David. She is singing the notes into his heart without moving her lips. And he is singing them back to her. We wrap them in our harmony.

We leave their house in radiance, taking some of their love, and some of Eileen's light with us back into our world of daily things. We feel the way sorrow can make itself at home in the heart, right alongside love. We circle in the dappled light of a giant maple, the peonies swaying their pink blossoms in the garden beds around us.

CHAPTER FOUR

STANDING CLOSE TO DEATH

What does it feel like to stand close to death? How do we remain calm, present and grounded when the breath of the dying and our own breath are mingled in the air?

The truth is, no matter how prepared we are, no matter how many sings we have attended, we never know what to expect once we are inside the room. Inside is the place where we stand beside the dying person. We are often in the circle of grieving family or friends. There is tremendous energy here. A waterfall of emotion and change. It may be the quietest place we have ever experienced and yet that quiet is charged with so much we cannot see or know. A whole life has come to rest at this place of transformation. As the dying person leaves the world, they leave a gaping hole that confuses those of us left. What once took up space physically and emotionally will be gone from the world as we know it. Being in this space calls us to be our highest selves. This feels true the moment we step over the threshold into someone else's story. There is no need to be known in here. It does not matter if the others around the bed notice us or know our names or even realize that we have been there to visit and sing. We are the most silent of presences. We are like the air. We come and go and leave behind a whisper of a breeze.

Stories

You Have All You Need

On the way to a sing for 92 year old Charlie dying in his home, I listen to an audio recording by John O'Donohue, an Irish writer/poet/philosopher/ex-Catholic priest, whose work has influenced my own. I hear him talk about how we have everything we need to make this journey alone when we're dying. His words ring true inside of me and when we gather in a circle on the front lawn of Charlie's house in town, I tell this to the singers. I tell them what I just heard and that no matter what we may believe in our own hearts, when we enter the space of Charlie's dying, we will believe that he has everything he needs to die well.

Charlie is in the front sunroom, full of light and family. His head is heavy on the pillow, mouth slightly open, eyes closed. Pockets hollow his mouth and eyes. Veins line blue, paper thin skin of his sunken face. Long pauses between breaths stop the rise and fall of his chest momentarily, as he labors to draw air into his lungs for a next breath. I pull a chair close to his bed to speak to him. "Charlie," I say, "There will be some people singing around you in a few minutes. You don't need to wake up. Just let the sounds wash over you. Stay where you are and rest in the music if you can." Nothing noticeable changes in Charlie. Sighs and audible breaths come from the family around him.

I retrieve the singers and we almost float into the room together, humming and finding our places in the sun around the bed. As we sing, I look at the faces of the singers, each one aglow, each one full of love and awe. Robin's eyes are at half mast. Mary Alice has a Buddha-like smile on her face and Peter stands as if in mountain pose in a yoga class. Tom is the mountain, strong and still. I sense the solid presence of each singer, believing in Charlie's wellness, in the rightness and beauty of his death as part of his life.

Peter leads us musically. His guidance is subtle but clear. His expertise and well-trained ear offers us the confidence we need to feel grounded and present in the face of so much coming at us: the smells of decay, the moans and cries of loved ones, the rattled breaths of Charlie.

We stand comfortably, firmly, feeling rooted in stance and sound. Our own breaths are full and easy and follow the notes out of our mouths where they meet and spiral into the songs that anoint this man on his journey. There is a confidence and ease among us, and a respect for this natural process of dying. I look at the faces of the family, twisted with grief and yet touched and opened to each other and to Charlie as he rests there in the center of all of us. We sing our songs to the rightness of his life, and to the end of it. We sing to say that he is tended on his journey. We sing, *"Life tend you on your journey. Love call me home."*

He is not alone. He has what he needs to make this passage. We believe it and we say it through our songs.

Rising Into the Stars

We pile into two cars, after rehearsing together with many other voices for three hours. Eight of us head into the starry March night to go to the place where Ellen rests on her death bed, her daughters around her. It feels late. Dark has settled over the Vermont countryside. The roads are empty except for our headlights.

We talk quietly on the way there. I am thinking about what we might sing, how we might begin, how I will make a connection with the family. And then I quiet the chatter in my head, ask prayerfully for guidance from the spirits, the angels, the energies that seem to lead us all so gracefully through these sing-overs. I clear my mind, decide to trust, notice the way the stars are so bright in the sky they seem closer than ever before.

We pass the sugarhouse, across from the old farm house, where this family has lived for generations. Men from the family and the farm hands are gathered around the evaporator where the sap boils furiously, thickening into sweet syrup. They feed the fire with slabs of dry wood, steam rises in the soft light of the sugarhouse and disappears into the stars, sweetening the night air. We park in front of the old barn where the cows are sleeping.

The front door to the house creaks as we slip inside. We take off our boots and shoes in the mud room. The walls are lined with cans of maple syrup. I go in ahead and alone to take in the scene, to talk to Ellen and her daughters. The house is deeply quiet. A low light burns in the kitchen and in Ellen's room, where she is propped comfortably in her bed. Pillows cushion her listing head. Blankets cover her. Her eyes are closed. Her breathing is raspy and uneven with long spaces between each one. She is a shell, a tiny bird. I am remembering how I used to see her in her white sneakers walking briskly in the morning chill along this valley road.

I stand at the foot of her bed. On either side of her, one daughter sits close, the other holds her hand. Their eyes are swollen and red rimmed from crying. But the low lights make everything look gentle and there is a sense of timelessness in this room. It could be early morning, midnight, midday, one hundred years ago. Time has slowed down. All there is, is here and now, this dying woman's breaths coming one labored inhalation at a time with long hesitant pauses in between. We have entered that place of edges and transitions, that place where mystery lives, where we have no answers, only our faith, only our love. We can almost feel the opening of a portal between this world and the next.

"Ellen," I say, "We have come to sing some quiet songs for you. You don't have to listen. You can simply let our harmonies wash over you. You can rest in our voices." I gather the others to form a tight circle in a room outside of the death room. There are maps from all over the world covering the walls like wallpaper. This feels surreal; the soft light, the steady slow rhythm of Ellen's final breaths, the quiet sobs of her daughters. The house smells of old wood and polish, of maple syrup and farm clothes, soap and lingering cooking smells, and above all else, the pungent, earthy smell of death and decay, of a body letting go.

We sing "There are Angels Hovering Round." And we can almost feel them, almost see them in this old farmhouse. I quietly check in with the daughters between songs. "How are you doing?" I whisper. One daughter nods. "Keep singing," the other says. "Please."

We share a sense of comfort, release, and grief flowing, as we sing, "O Sing to Me of Heaven," *Let music charm me last on earth, and greet me first in heaven. There'll be no sorrow there. In heaven above, where all is love, there'll be no sorrow there.* We chant, "Khvalytie," a liturgical Russian orthodox piece full of Alleluias. *Alleluia, Alleluia* are holy words sung with bowed heads.

We are a tightly tuned circle of voices. As a group, we grow quiet, slow down together. We are singing one song. We become one with everything; the night, this old farmhouse, all of those who have been born or have died here, the stars, the steam from the sugarhouse rising into the night sky. She will rise up on this steam, I think. She will rise up into the glory of the stars tonight. We sing, *"How could anyone ever tell you, you were anything less than beautiful. How deeply you're connected to my soul."*

Finally, we tiptoe quietly out of the room. In the mud room, we slip on our boots and hold hands in a sacred circle. I look from face to face, amazed and deeply grateful. I love every face. Death has opened our hearts to life. Death has been our teacher again.

As we drive back past the sugarhouse, sparks are flying into the night, the steam dissolving into stars, the sweet boil of sap changing into syrup, transforming one thing into another. The mystery of death is still upon our lips, as fresh as the songs we were privileged to share with this old Vermont family on a starry night in March.

FIVE

CHANGE

How do we know if the singing changes anything? We don't know, of course. When we attend a vigil sing, when someone is very close to the end of their life, we often witness them laboring towards death. There is work involved in the dying process. Good work. Natural work. Work that leads to transition and change.

During my years of practicing midwifery, I guided women through labor with my quiet presence. This was my greatest gift as a midwife, to be able to be there in full awareness, capable, ready to respond if needed, but also able to stay out of the way of a healthy process. Hands off, heart and mind alert and ready. We know how to give birth and we know how to die. Or from the perspective of the new life coming into the world, we know how to be born. And we know how to die. These are healthy life processes. We are never so strong as when we are following the natural way of life and trusting in the wellness that supports it.

It might seem strange to think of a dying person as being well, or strong. But when a person has arrived at the threshold between life and death, and is working toward letting go of the body, all else falls away and there is only this left. This is the work of dying. Letting go of resistance. Accepting and allowing. Ease and grace. This is what we look upon and this is what we sing to. Our songs seem to soften the breath, smooth the edges, quiet the fear, lessen the resistance. Sometimes it's simply our presence, the fact that we have come to witness and be with someone, that offers strength and comfort. Sometimes the changes we see are subtle. Sometimes we have no idea if we were heard at all. Other times, there is no question that a change occurs as a result of our visit.

We don't expect anything. And we don't pretend to know what is needed or what works or even what this singing is about. We do it because it feels good. It feels like grace.

Stories

❦

Epiphany

When the call came in the middle of a weekday from hospice to sing for a dying woman, I gathered a group to meet in the lobby of Pine Heights nursing home. Evelyn had requested a sing for her ninety year old mother, Caroline. "She doesn't have long," she told us.

We found Caroline in the hospice room at the end of the hall. In her bed, covered in flannel, eyes closed, her breathing was slow and labored and she was unresponsive to my voice. She looked peacefully and deeply asleep.

Evelyn was sitting at the far end of the room on the couch provided for family. I asked her if she might like to come over and sit beside her mother while we sang. "No thanks," she told us. "I'm just going to rest here." Her eyes were red rimmed and creases crossed her cheek where her face had been pressed into the edge of the pillow. Evelyn looked wilted. We had been told, during our initial contact with hospice, that there was a difficult dynamic between this mother and daughter. You could almost see it in the set of her jaw, the tightness around her mouth, the way her shoulders were set. She wore a wrinkled oversized shirt. She wore her weariness and her sorrow. "If you change your mind, you are welcome to come sit beside your mom while we sing," I said. She lay down on the couch and turned her back to the room.

Six singers positioned ourselves around Caroline's bed and started with a gentle song. I placed myself close to the head of the bed, but with a clear view of Evelyn. I wanted to keep my eye on her. As we sang I watched her uncurl a bit. She turned around, sat up and let the weight of her head fall into the palms of her hands. I walked over to her as the singers continued and touched her shoulder. "Would you like to come over now," I offered her my hand. She shook her head no again but shortly after, she rose and moved to her mother's bed. We parted way for her to climb into bed with her mother as we continued to sing, *"There'll be no sorrow there. In heaven above where all is love, there'll be no sorrow there."* Evelyn buried her face into her mother's chest and wept while we sang. She held nothing back. She wrapped her arms around her mother and rocked her and cried. She gently rested her hand over her mother's heart. She sobbed and we sang and sang until we felt it was enough. Evelyn's unexpected grief had reached a point of saturation. She needed a rest from her tears and time alone with her dying mother.

Keeping ourselves present in the face of Evelyn's heart-wrenching emotions had both opened and filled us. We left carrying some of the weight of it in our own hearts. We left Evelyn in bed with her mother to stay with her until she died.

In our closing circle, we agreed something had changed between mother and daughter during our singing. We all felt it but could not know what it was or honestly name it. We tried to speak of what it felt like. Healing. Resistance into acceptance. Release of emotion. A lifetime of grief letting go. Love. Ultimately, love.

Many months later, I met Evelyn on the sidewalk in town. Piles of dirty snow were melting into the street on a warm day in early spring. Buds were swollen on the branches of maple trees. Birds flew over our heads and a sea of people passed around us as Evelyn pulled me into an unexpected embrace. She said she was grateful for the opportunity to tell me that our sing for her mother had been a healing for them. "It was an epiphany," she said. Later she shared her experience with me in writing, all of those things we could not have known were changing as we stood singing around mother and daughter. We had been witnesses to a greater change and healing than we could have imagined. Here are Evelyn's words:

> I just gave up trying to be strong or indifferent and came over. The presence of so much benign attention from the singers, along with the beautiful music, opened a channel to my soul that I had resolutely blocked off ever since my early childhood. I can tell you now, nearly seven years later, that this was the only time I cried over my mother's death. I was crying for nearly sixty years of lost opportunity, for my mother's selfish neglect of my needs and refusal to love me, for my own selfish (or defensive) reluctance to love her and attend to her needs, and for a number of other losses, including the very recent and very raw loss of my marriage of 27 years.
>
> It wasn't long after your visit that I made a crucial realization. My mother was embarking on one of the most significant transitions of a person's lifetime, yet

over the years she had essentially made me responsible for huge parts of her own soul. She had often
made it explicitly clear that her happiness and sense
of self-worth were largely dependent on me; for
decades I had felt the burden of taking care of her
emotional well-being. Now she was about to die. But
how could she make such a momentous journey with
only part of her soul?

I remember my head snapping up with the epiphany that I had been care-taking her soul for decades
and that she needed it back, now! I reached out my
arms and scooped up all the scattered little fragments
of her poor shattered soul and, with gentle respect,
returned the enormous load to her. I piled up all the
bits I'd been carrying around on her chest, where
they could return to her through her heart. I've never
felt so relieved in my life.

That moment freed me forever. When she died a
day or two later, taking her entire soul with her, I
experienced such a sense of a weight lifted that for
months I felt like I was floating. I'd heard of "weight
off the shoulders" before, of course; it's a cliche in
our culture, but I was shocked at how much lighter—
literally, physically lighter—I felt.

Evelyn's words settled into my own soul. We know so little
about the effects of singing at the bedside. Inside the room of the

dying, we learn to trust the process and allow ourselves to be guided by truth and directed by our hearts. If we leave a sing with even the smallest bit of that grace, then perhaps the subtle gift of change we hope for occurs beyond the bedside, in our own daily lives and relationships.

SIX

GATHERING

The deathbed is a place of slowed time. When you sit with someone who is dying, it's as if you have entered a space where time bends at the edge, between the world we know and somewhere else. It is the same kind of time-lost place that is experienced at a birth. During my years of practicing midwifery, I experienced many days and nights of stretched time. Sleepless, long nights could seem only a few minutes long or maybe a few years long. Time is simply a different experience when you are standing close to the passing in or out of a soul. It is no wonder that it shimmers here beside the death bed. It is no wonder that when we start to sing here, the gathering of loved ones happens naturally.

When the singing starts, it is like a call to prayer, like chimes or bells ringing to summon people into a church or temple. The sound of voices in harmony naturally invites this drawing in. It invites people to pause, calls them to listen. It is an offering to stop whatever they are doing and come to the bedside to be with their loved one.

The reason we are called is to call others with our songs. This is a sacred moment, this time of gathering.

Stories

❦

Love Around You

Imagine, if at the end of your life, you feel well enough to have the ones you choose around you in a flow of everyday life: chopping vegetables, stirring pots, making coffee, gossiping, washing dishes, folding sheets and towels. Imagine the younger ones outside, running around with balls and frisbees and dogs. The phone is ringing because friends are calling to connect with you. You are resting on your pillow, covered in folds of flannel comforters, sunlight is flooding the room. The warmth is making you drowsy so you drift in and out of this lively scene easily and often, resting in the sounds of daily life.

It was this way when five of us arrived in the middle of a Sunday to sing for Jim. His quiet home was at the end of a dirt road in Vermont. The place was pulsing with life, inside and out. Family had come from far and away to gather and say goodbye to Grandpa Jim. The grown children had arrived, children of all ages from adults down to the newest great granddaughter in-arms.

Children paused in their play as we arrived, but went quickly back to the world of reunited cousins as soon as they realized we were only more adults coming to see grandpa. We were welcomed in by a daughter. The aroma of coffee wafted from the kitchen. We declined the offer of spice cake. Someone took our jackets. We settled in as quietly as possible amidst what felt like a family holiday. I asked if I could meet Jim before we sang.

Jim was alone in his room when I went in to sit with him for a minute. He offered me a kind smile. I could see that it was an effort for him to talk, so I just told him a few things without asking any questions. I told him there were a few people who had come to sing for him. I told him he needn't try to stay awake for our singing, and that in fact, if we put him to sleep that would be just fine. I told him we didn't expect an audience, we were not performing. And he could receive it in any way that offered him rest. There was nothing we needed or expected from him or from anyone else who might come to listen. He nodded, smiled, and laying his head back, closed his eyes. I left him to go and get the others.

Back in the main house, the children had been called inside and adults had collected in the living room. They all wanted to be with Grandpa/Dad/Jim for the sing. They filed quietly into his bedroom. There must have been twenty bodies in that room. Some of the smaller children climbed right onto the bed and lay down alongside Grandpa Jim. Everyone found a place. Some sat on the floor, some on chairs, some on the bed. A few people leaned against the wall or in the doorway. We stood close together to form a semi-circle around the foot of the bed. Knowing how to be quiet inside of ourselves before we start to sing helps to lessen the physical space we take up in the room. We become energetically smaller. We do this by watching our breath. Being calm. Having a still mind. Moving deliberately and slowly. We have learned how to be comfortable with silence, before we sing and in-between songs. In this way, we can hear better. We can listen from a deeper well. Patience becomes part of the song.

Our quieting reached the family. Making time for this sing had gathered them to be with Jim, to acknowledge together that he would die soon, to share their sadness about this loss, so hard to speak of. We sang the hymn "Be Not Afraid." We sang, "There's a Light." *There's a light, there's a light, in the darkness, and the dark of the night cannot harm us. We can trust not to fear, for our comfort is near. There's a light in the darkness.*

Silence lingered in between the songs. You could almost hear the collective breath of family. We sang for about forty minutes. Boxes of tissues were passed around the room. Jim had his eyes closed, but on his face was a peaceful smile. His face was relaxed and his breathing was easy. He was at the center of his loving family, looking beyond here to a place that beckoned, a place no one else could see.

After we ended our sing and eased out of the room on the sounds of our hums, the party re-started. The children busted out of the room back to the yard. The women, still blowing noses, rearranged themselves in the kitchen, chatting easily. One son stayed behind with his dad and called me back into the room. Jim wanted to say thank you. I took his hand and found his gaze. "You seem so happy," I said to him. "Wouldn't you be," he asked, "with all of this love around you?"

Thanksgiving

It was a dark, cold, December evening when we were called to sing for Lucy. There was no further treatment for the metastasized breast cancer that would take her life. She had come home to die with her family around her. They had put off Thanksgiving until they could bring Lucy home, and so this evening was the preparation for their Thanksgiving time. The house was well lit when we arrived. Five of us climbed up onto the wooden porch and tried the locked door. We could see inside through the window, and watched a kitchen full of people, laughing and talking. Pies were cooling on the counter. Many hands were cutting up squash and peeling potatoes. A television was on somewhere in the house. Children were running through the rooms. We knocked again and again. At first timidly, then harder and louder until someone finally came to the door, apologizing for not hearing us. "It is noisy in here!" Lucy's daughter said. "I'm terribly sorry. Come on in. It's so cold out there."

As the other singers took off boots and coats and found a place in the mudroom to leave piles of winter garb, I went in ahead to locate Lucy. I found her lying on the couch in the family room. The kitchen, still bustling with activity, was behind us. The room was cozy with soft dark furniture. Lucy was settled into a warm couch corner, books of prayers beside her. She reached for my hand when I kneeled beside the couch. Her eyes brightened as she told me she was not afraid to die and that it was her strong faith that carried her through her journey with cancer. Her belief in God was helping her find strength and courage as she faced her death. She was beautiful, almost translucent with pale skin and wisps of reddish grey hair splayed across her pillow. She wore a loose cotton shift. Her hands looked tender and young. Soft spoken but very clear, she seemed frail and strong, all at once.

No one else in the family seemed to know or mind that we had come, so the singers and I moved around Lucy to sing, no matter what else was going on in the house. The three women—two altos, one soprano, knelt down beside the couch. The two men, a bass and a tenor, stood behind us. We started to sing, *"I will guide thee, with mine eyes. All the way from earth to heaven, I will guide thee, with mine eyes."* Lucy closed her eyes gently.

The family sounds grew quiet. They put down knives and spoons. They moved towards the family room. The children grew quiet and came to perch on other couches or the floor. Lucy's husband sat at her feet and rested his hand on her leg. The daughters and sons-in-law found seats on the couches. If quiet was something you could hold in your hand, this quiet would be held in cupped palms, to be poured over the heads of this family like a baptism. It was a call to gather. To slow down, pause, and notice where we all were.

The entire family gathered around Lucy, listened to the songs, and listened while she spoke about each song and how it affirmed her faith. Tears were shed in reverence. This sing became a moment of giving thanks among this family, for Lucy and her life and for each other.

The Real Funeral

The call from Oona, to sing for her mother Bridget, came in the middle of a Saturday. "Come as soon as possible," she said. Six singers changed plans and drove to the hospital to meet in the lobby and prepare ourselves. We shared what we knew about this tiny Irish woman who was at the end of her long life. She was a force in her family, now gathering to say goodbye.

We sang through a song as a way to bring ourselves together. Being called out of our lives to come to a bedside asks our highest selves to arrive here, in this place, now. We reminded each other, through breath and song, to let go of all we had just been doing and all we might do next. There was no place else to be, nothing else to be doing in this moment. In that state of mind and heart, we entered the room where Bridget was dying and her family had come to be with her.

Before our arrival they had been scattered throughout the hospital, at the coffee shop or out walking the grounds. Now the room was brimming with sons and daughters, grandchildren and great grandchildren. They sat on the bed, on the floor, on the few chairs along the wall. We found our place in the small entryway from hallway into room, stood shoulder to shoulder and sang to this loving family.

Bridget was a small being of breath and bones beneath her blankets. Oxygen mask and tubes could not hide the way her gaze lingered a few moments upon each beloved face around her. Oona asked us to sing some songs to help her to let go. *"I'll Fly Away,"* we sang. And *"Fields are ripe and harvest ready, who will bear my soul away."* The family took turns laying down beside Bridget, holding her and weeping, full voice keening, while we sang. It was an extraordinary display of grief.

Often there is a point in our singing when we realize that the family has reached a saturation moment. They need a rest from the well of grief opened by the singing. And so we change the tone a bit, sing something to ease the heart. Maybe a song in another language or a chant with soothing sounds. When Oona asked us if we could sing something a little more uplifting, we knew we had reached that time of fullness.

Often a song will choose itself around a death bed. "Parting Glass"—not exactly uplifting—somehow wanted to be the next song. *But since it falls, upon my lot, that I should rise and you should not: then I'll gently rise, and I'll softly call: Goodnight and joy be with you all.*

Bridget's face softened into a glow. Her breath, labored and audible until now, grew steady and quiet. So did her surrounding family. If they could move physically closer to her, they did. They gathered. The thread that held them all together had been pulled by the music, the words, the light in Bridget's smiling eyes, and they gathered like pleats on a skirt.

Our singing is a call to presence. The voice, vulnerable as an instrument of the body, calls others to attention and invites them to settle into the heart. As we sang for Bridget, we watched this family open and close, grieve together and grieve individually. We watched Bridget watching it too. In the center of the heart of her family, wrapped up in song and cries of the broken hearted, love spoke to

Bridget. Love filled the room. "Love call me home," we sang, and it did just that.

Weeks later, I met Bridget's daughter, Oona, in town. The funeral had taken place, she told me. Family and friends had come. Prayers were read and stories were shared. The priest spoke and read passages from the bible. "She has been called home to God," he told the church full of people.

"The funeral was good," Oona told me, "but it didn't really do for us what your singing did. That time brought us together, to grieve as a family. That singing in her hospital room," Oona said, "was the real funeral for us."

SEVEN

THE SHAPE OF FAMILY

Understanding and accepting that we will see and be among every kind of family as we go out into the community to offer our service of bedside singing is essential to the heart of our practice. Some people come from strong intact families, where the land and house is passed down from generation to generation. Family holidays and traditions are shared and celebrated. There are no divorces or separations, parents and grandparents stay together for life. Children are stable and live nearby. We sing in the old farmhouse where the husband sits with his wife of 70 years as she is dying. The grown children and grandchildren are in the room. This is beautiful to witness, but this is rare and this is the exception.

More often we see relationships that have changed along with the definition of family. We see the man who dies alone in the nursing home with no one visiting him at the end of his life. We see the woman with her third husband and the daughter in-law from the second marriage at her bedside. We see siblings who don't talk. We sing for a gay man while his lifetime partner holds his hand and cries. We sing for a woman who lives independently and considers her friends chosen family. They gather around her to help her die.

We are given opportunities, again and again, to practice how not to pass judgement but to look on in wonder and with curiosity.

Most of all, we are invited to accept what is, as it is, without our own decided beliefs clouding what we see. Love takes different forms and changes like the clouds. We learn to see the love at the bedside. There are no rules about the way it looks in order for it to be called love. We define "Family" by looking at what we see and asking our hearts what it means to be a part of one.

Witnessing and being among another's family as a bedside singer allows each of us a window into our own personal relationship with family. We might leave a sing with a sense of nostalgia and longing for what we don't have, or what we may have lost, or we may leave feeling a sense of gratitude for our own lives and loves, in whatever shape they take. Time allows the integration of this practice and all it reveals, and affects the way we see the world through our eyes, mind and heart.

Stories

꽃

To Die at Home

We surround a bed where someone is dying. For now we are the ones singing. For now, we are standing or sitting around the bed, looking in at someone else's journey. But for each of us these questions stand with us. How will I die? Will I be curious? Will I be afraid? Will I be alone? Will I be in pain or comfortable? Where will I be?

When we call our family home to be with us, when we choose and are able to die in our own bed, in our home, within the flow of life, we are truly living until we die. We are part of the natural rhythm and flow of birth, life and death. Perhaps the transition from body to spirt becomes more gentle. And hopefully, the grief of those left behind is eased. We sing around this gentleness, ever in awe and always full of gratitude for this mystery of living and dying.

Marilyn is settled into her bed in the home where she has lived for fifty years. At 92 years old, she has seen family come and go from this old house. Her family has moved her bedroom to the first floor, through the brightly lit country kitchen at the end of the hall. The room is full of windows and since we are here at dusk in winter, we can see and feel the fading light in the room as we sing. Mike, Marilyn's husband of 70 years, leans back in a cushioned chair in the corner of the room. Two grown daughters sit beside the bed, close enough to reach for her hands or stroke her arm. Their son stands near his father. A granddaughter in her early twenties with darkened hair and tattoos on her arm, sits near the head of the bed, closest to her grandmother. Behind her a guitar leans against the wall.

Marilyn's eyes are closed. Her breathing is steady and easy. She looks comfortable, as though she is sleeping soundly, yet she looks like a person who is close to dying. The skin on her face has begun to lose shape and fit more closely around the bones of cheeks and jowl. Her body seems to be shrinking, collapsing in on itself. And yet, because the family is here, and love and grief and stories are flowing around her, the restful sleep of Marilyn's dying is comfortable and pain free. We are witnessing her final letting go and breaths of release. There is great beauty here at this bedside.

I ask the granddaughter if she plays the guitar and if she has been singing for her grandmother. "Yes," she says. She's a little bit tipsy from the wine the family has been drinking, good wine they make from the grapes they grow. She sings along with us, loudly, and in her own personal key, but there is a lift of the corner of Marilyn's mouth and there is a broad smile on Mike's face as his eyes go between his granddaughter to his wife and then over us. He is drinking in the whole room. The whole room is filled with tears, song, love, wine, family. This is a room where someone is dying. This is life. This is letting go with tenderness and warmth.

As we ease our way out of Marilyn's room, Mike pulls himself out of his soft chair to follow us. We are trying to slip away quietly. Still humming the last song, we attempt to leave the family together in the sweetness we have just witnessed. We take ourselves out of the way of what the family might share in the aftermath of our singing. Mike, however, follows us out. He so clearly wants to say something to us before we leave. With tears in his eyes, his voice full of emotion, he tells us, "That was the most beautiful send off anyone could ever have. Tell me, how do you say goodbye to someone you have shared your life with?" We have no answer of course, but we make a space for him in our circle and sing one more song to say, *"There are angels hovering 'round, Let all who hear them come."* It gives him just enough courage to return to the bedside and sit closer to his beloved wife as she prepares to leave the life they have shared for so long.

Forgiveness Brings Light

August 5th 2011 was Joseph's birthday. This would be his last one, and the celebration was as much for his pending death as it was for his birth. We were called two days ahead of this birthday sing and given a description of Joe, along with the story of how he ended up in his daughter's home in southern Vermont at the end of his life. We were told that he had been living in Tucson, Arizona, in the late stages of Alzheimer's, when his fourth wife left him. He had not spoken to his daughter Trish for the past twelve years, but her heart led her to Arizona to fetch her father and bring him back to Vermont to live out his days in her home, among her family of four. Trish and her husband, MJ, were raising their two daughters in a modest split level ranch on a back road in a quiet town. There was not a lot of extra space for her estranged father with Alzheimer's, but they made room for him. We learned that Joe had sung in a church choir before he became too afflicted by the Alzheimer's. When Joe could no longer remember much else, he still remembered the words to his favorite songs.

We found Joe in a room down the narrow hallway from where we entered the house. It was mid-day when we came to sing. We were greeted by Trish and MJ's two girls, spinning and twirling in their summer skirts and bare feet. Alice and Abbi were eager to follow us into their grandfather's room. They understood why we were there and that this day was grandpa's birthday. They also understand that he was dying and that soon he wouldn't be with them, this strange man who didn't know who they were or where he was. This grandfather their mother went to find and brought home to take care of. He had been living with them for twenty months before he had taken to his bed a few weeks before. By the time we got there to sing for him, he had not had any food or water for four days and was in the deep state of elsewhere.

The house reflected a busy life, clean laundry being folded, snacks in a bowl for the girls, games and puzzles on the table alongside medical supplies. Everywhere were signs of exhaustion as Trish juggled her time between care of her family and her dying father.

Joe's room was quiet and clean. Beside his bed, we met Grandma Alice, who sat and held his hand. She offered me her other hand as I went in ahead of the others to meet Joe. Alice was the grandmother of the girls, little Alice's namesake, mother of Trish and first wife of Joe. She was remarried, she told us, to Jack. But here she was at Joe's bedside, tending him, keeping vigil, talking to him quietly, singing, praying, being with him in stillness. This was family, I thought, in every sense of the word.

Forgiveness makes the heart light. Our first song called the others into the room. The girls climbed onto the bed. Trish took her father's other hand. Trish's husband hovered in the doorway. We all felt lightness as we chose songs for Joe and the family. They all joined in the singing, adding harmonies, as we sang over and around Joe in his silent place. We sang "Blessed Quietness" and "Love Call Me Home." We sang "All Through the Night" and "Over the Rainbow." Trish requested "The 23rd Psalm." *The Lord is my shepherd, I have all I need.* We sang for and with these women and girls around Joe for an hour. We laughed and cried and sang for Joe on his birthday, the day before he would die.

Almost two years later, Alice called us again. This time we were invited to sing for her husband Jack in the nursing home where he had been living with end stage dementia. He was in decline, she told us, and the family would love to have the singers come.

We found Jack in his room in a relaxed sleep. This surprised Alice, as she had expected him to be awake and in the dining room for dinner hour. Six of us fit ourselves into his room, along with Alice, Trish, her husband, and the girls carrying yellow balloons and bouquets of wildflowers. We started out with quiet, soothing songs around Jack's bed as he slept, careful not to disturb him. Alice surprised us this time when she requested one of Jack's favorites, the rousing shape note hymn "New Jerusalem." I would not have selected that song, but there are times when the family steers and we follow. "New Jerusalem" woke Jack up, to the utter delight of everyone around him. His eyes popped open. It was his turn to be surprised. A wide grin spread across his face, to our relief, and the whole feeling in the room changed from reverent to celebratory as we pulled out all of the lively spirited songs the family wanted to sing with us. Acceptance, love, joy, gratitude. We felt waves of almost touchable emotion between all of us that day in Jack's room. We were witness, once again, to this family's heart, as we sang to send Jack on his way.

A Social Visit With Martha and Leo

We sing in so many different situations. I often say we sing along a spectrum. At the beginning of the spectrum are social visits, where a person is not close to dying. At the far end, someone is within hours of taking their last breath; or what we refer to as vigil sings.

In the case of a social sing, the patient may be receiving services from an early care program through their local hospice. The patient in a case like this is fully alive and the purpose of our visit is to bring spirit and joy through our singing. Often people will sing along. Sometimes, this kind of sing is as much or even more for the family members than for the patient we are called to visit. Families who are caring for an aging parent or parents are often exhausted and in need of some outside connection.

Whenever we sing in a situation that is more social, it's always a good idea to try to communicate to the primary caretaker that we are also available for a different kind of sing as things change. We have chants or reverent music that can be sung while someone is sleeping. We can arrive and leave without any need for interaction. During the social sing, it's important to sing at least one or two songs to calm things down between songs, but also, to demonstrate to the family the kind of soothing music we have in our repertoire.

Less than four years before our visit, Victor and Julie had moved to an old Victorian house in a small town in New Hampshire. They had been constantly busy with construction and refurbishing projects, doing most of the work themselves, leaving very little time to explore the area, or to develop any kind of social life. At the heart of their project was the renovation of the old carriage house, transformed into a home for Victor's parents, Martha and Leo.

Martha and Leo had been living in Colorado when Martha was diagnosed with Alzheimer's disease. By the time we met her, her disease had advanced to the point where she could no longer be left alone. Martha could be easily aroused, we had been warned, based on an incident at the adult daycare center when another woman annoyed Martha and she responded with a good right handed punch. We would be mindful when choosing songs, alert to how the music might affect her. We would also be aware of how gently we approached her, trying not to be disruptive with our arrival.

Victor and Julie had done some research before moving their parents into a new home. They discovered that certain colors worked to calm the patient with Alzheimer's. They learned that it helped when moving a person out of their home, to replicate what was already familiar as much as possible. They set the chairs, two recliners, side by side facing the television. The kitchen was laid out in simple order. Martha's paintings, bright and lively watercolors, were hung on the walls of the bedroom. The flow of rooms, placement of furniture, display of art and objects, contrast of colors, all details were carefully thought out and offered simple comfort and beauty as well as easier navigation of spaces. Sunlight filled the rooms, softened by light, airy curtains.

Leo's needs were considered as well. Victor met us in the driveway and led us through what was soon-to-be a woodworking shop for Leo. This led to an attached greenhouse where there were already pots of tomatoes on shelves that Leo had started in early March. He came out to see who had arrived when he heard our voices and learned for the first time that we had come to sing for him. Leo is eighty two years old, in good health and of sound mind. Yet he is a bit lost and confused in a new home and town and with his wife in a place he can not follow. Though she is sitting beside him in her recliner, she is miles away from him. The loneliness showed through his delight at having visitors. When he realized we were here to sing for him and Martha, he beamed and then pulled me into a hug as if we were old friends. Leo, it turned out, was a guitar player and singer of old folk songs. I laughed and hugged him back, just as delighted.

Martha seemed to know we had come to visit her. "Would you like to hear some singing?" we asked. "Oh no," she said as a huge smile followed. Victor sat himself down right beside her. He smiled too and translated. "She means Yes of course." And so we began with "I Still Have Joy." If a face could open, Martha's did. Her brows raised. Her eyes widened. Her mouth made an OH. Her feet danced where they rested. Leo also looked this way, with less child-like wonder, but he wore a similar look of surprise and delight when we started to sing, *"I still have joy, I still have joy, after all the things I've been through I still have joy."* "Okay then!" Martha exclaimed. There was nothing to do but laugh.

Our visit with Martha and Leo, Victor and Julie, was light-hearted and social. No one was dying here. There had been significant change and loss, and now adjustment. This lovely couple who had spent the last years fixing up an old house and making a home for their aging parents, were hungry for social connection. There was a feeling of welcome and gratitude among us all as we sang for almost an hour, checking in to see if everyone was still settled and okay with the singing. We watched Victor take his mother's hand as we sang the words, *"The thing that makes you beautiful is in your eyes."* He didn't let it go until we were done. We watched Leo blow Martha a kiss from his chair. Leo sang along on "Wonderful World," "I'll Fly Away," "Over the Rainbow" and "You Are My Sunshine." Martha sang along too. We chose songs to say what we wanted to say, to invite others to sing with us, and to bring joy into the home. Every song seemed just right. "Would you like another song Martha?" we asked. "No!" she said. And we sang one.

Later, after we were offered black walnut cranberry cookies and shown (at Leo's insistence) the collection of buffalo furniture Leo had brought with him, I managed a quiet moment with Victor. I wanted him to know that we could come in a different capacity, sing at any time, offer quieter songs while someone slept, be a smaller group. He understood. For now, this time, this sing, was just what was needed for this whole family.

Departure felt like old friends leaving after a wonderful visit. Leo followed us out to the greenhouse to hug each one of us in turn and say thank you. When I gifted him with our CD's, the tears that were already brimming leaked out and he brushed them away with the back of his hand and shook his head. What can we know of another's life? What can we know of another's heart?

As we drove out of the driveway, there was Leo, curtains pulled back, waving us away through the window, Martha settled quietly and happily in her chair behind him.

When Does the Singing Come?

Not everyone is a candidate for a bedside sing. Not everyone wants strangers around them, singing songs, while they are dying. We never assume or impose anything. We go when and where we are invited to sing.

Snooy always had clear ideas about what she wanted. Being an indecisive person myself, it was one of the things I most loved and admired and even envied about my beloved friend. She also knew what she didn't want. One of the things she made quite clear about her dying wishes was that for deeply personal reasons, she didn't want singing around her as she labored towards her final breath. Although she loved music in her life and singing along with Leon's guitar playing had always been a central part of our extended community's gatherings, she did not wish to have the Hallowell singers come and sing songs that she might not have chosen. And so I never offered.

Snooy had her mind made up about so many parts of her journey. She astonished those of us who were witness to her final days. During many trips to Dartmouth with her for oncology appointments or treatments or procedures that might prolong her life, we watched in awe as she became her own best self-advocate, asking researched questions about her cancer and the latest drugs and tests, or more often, educating the hospital staff with facts she had learned on her own. She always knew exactly what was being done to her and why. Snooy was well versed in everything there was to know about multiple myeloma, the cancer that would take her life anyway. The singing came later, at just the perfect moment, in its right time.

Six women surrounded Snooy's death bed watching for the next breath that never came. We watched in silence, waiting for her chest to rise once more, and when the realization hit us that she had died, we fell into each other's arms weeping. It was as if we felt the physical impact of her passing in our own bodies and spirits. What could we possibly understand, those of us who are still grounded in this world, of what happens when a spirit leaves a body? I felt love there in our weeping, in our sobs and wails and arms around each other. In the tears that would flow for days and weeks and months to come, that would open our hearts to our own living again and again.

We unplugged her, took out needles, covered her with a warm blanket, rested her head on the pillow. We drove to her house to choose clothes from her drawers and closet, to cut flowers from her garden, to pick out favorite earrings and a few items to be cremated along with her body. We brought lavender soap and a soft washcloth and towel.

Back at the hospital, the room now magically filled with the flowers she could not have around her in her illness, four of us, one a sister, one a niece who shares Snooy's birthday, and two close friends, undressed her and washed her lovingly from head to foot. We lifted her arms, washed her breasts, between her legs, each finger, each toe. We rolled her over to run the soft warm cloth over her back, buttocks, legs. And then we dressed her. We lifted, held, cooed and cried. We pulled on her softest, favorite purple cotton shirt and sweatpants. A colorful scarf. Sparkling glass earrings. We arranged her on pillows, soft, purple and beautiful, and covered her with delphiniums, lilies, bee balm, astilby and meadow rue. The room smelled like lavender soap, flowers and death. We opened the door to invite the men and others who were waiting to reenter. We had performed an ancient ritual and our hands had been guided.

At first we were quiet. Reverent. Looking at the body of this woman we had all loved. This woman who had been the reason for so many of our connections. She had given us endless advice and guidance over the years. Her home had been a center for many of our gatherings or drop in visits. She had woven this community of friends together, and now we were here to say goodbye and share our grief. In silence we stood around her bed. Leon's guitar rested against the wall. I looked at it, looked at him. Why not? Why not now? This was the time for the singing.

We started out quietly. "On the Wings of the Snow White Dove." "I'll Fly Away." We sang softly, with reverence and respect. We didn't want to disturb her, or the energy in the room. But as we sang, our spirits lifted and the songs started to come and come. It was as if Snooy was asking, as she always had, sing this one or that one. "My Little Runaway". Now we were laughing and crying and singing with great open voices and joy. It couldn't have been more perfect. For two hours, while we waited for the man from Eternal Flame Crematorium to arrive, we sang song after song that Snooy had loved in her lifetime. The music filled us, pulled us together, soothed our hearts. And somehow, deep inside of myself where truth and beliefs live, I knew the songs lifted Snooy's spirit to wherever it was she needed or wanted to go on that day of her dying.

Later, back at Snooy's house, we found the scrap of paper among her instructions that listed the songs she wanted sung at her memorial service party. Every one of the songs we sang around her bed that day was on the list.

Children at the Bedside

Summer is a challenging time to answer incoming calls for Hallowell. Although we have twelve leaders, those people who are trained to be in the role of relating to the family and the person we are called to visit, summer schedules often leave us limited and leaders are hard to come by. This is how it was when the call came to sing for Luella. There was no question we needed to get to her bedside. I had my grandson Fin with me and no back-up for his care that day. There was no choice but to bring him along to the sing.

Our relationship with Luella began eight years ago, when we were called to her ninety one year old husband, Harry's, bedside. Grace Cottage is a small country hospital, with a room reserved for hospice patients at the far end of the hall. The room is a simple hospital room, small but brightly lit with windows looking out into the flower gardens. There is a large adjoining room with couches, tables and a small kitchen area. Here the family can regroup and rest or, weather permitting, move outside onto the deck where there are chairs and a picnic table for their use during the many hours they are likely to be there.

We arrived on that day to find a dying man in the center of a living family. As Harry rested brittle bones of his shrinking body, the family ordered pizza. He dozed on and off, head listing on the pillow in his hospital bed. The children colored and giggled in the next room. The room stretched to fit a son and four daughters, their husbands and children, several in-laws, two dogs and some grandchildren. The children seemed happy to be together. They were fed and entertained. And yet they understood, the way children do, that something significant was happening in the room where their grandfather lay with his eyes closed, no longer answering their questions.

On the dresser in Harry's room was an urn of ashes, the remains of Harry and Luella's son, a loss the family spoke about openly.

Our singing called the family to the bedside. The children quieted and moved towards Harry. Luella sat beside him, holding his hand, whispering in his ear while we sang. Her own manicured hands were noticeably white and soft, blue veins reaching towards slender fingers, respectable pink polish on filed nails. She was dressed as if she were on her way to church. Almost formally. Yet there was nothing formal about the emotions of love and loss we witnessed as she sat at her husband's bedside while he lay dying.

A week later, we filled a long pew on the side of the church to sing at Harry's funeral. The family welcomed us into the heart of their loss and grief.

Over the next few years, I came to know Luella better. She was a natural lady, carefully and elegantly adorned. She chose quiet colors that perfectly matched, a skirt with a simple top or sweater with pearl buttons or a bit of lace. She could easily have worn a hat with a pin or white gloves. Luella spoke softly and moved with grace.

She looked directly at the person she was speaking to, or listening to, with gentle brown eyes. Her eyes were a place you wanted to stay for a very long time.

Luella never forgot that we sang for her beloved husband. For years after Harry's death, we saw Luella at the residential assisted living home where she lived. When we gathered residents in the parlor to hear us sing, Luella showed up and chose a Victorian chair with arms. She draped her shawl carefully over the back. She closed her eyes while she listened to the music. Afterward, she called me over, took my hand, and pulled me into her eyes. She told me how much it meant to her and her family that we sang for Harry. I was struck each time by the soft strength of her. Even as it became clear that communication was becoming confusing for Luella due to loss of vision and hearing, she spoke to us of our sing for Harry. And she talked about her son who lived in Ashfield and wondered if I had ever been there. I had, I told her, and I loved the town. We made plans to meet there for lunch someday. That day never came.

The summer day we were called to sing for Luella, in the same room where we had sung for Harry, I gathered a small group, packed up some things to keep Fin busy for an hour, and Tom and I drove to Grace cottage to meet the others. I explained to Fin, seven years old at the time, that we were going to visit a woman who was dying and that we would be singing for her to help her die in a gentle way. I had packed him a bag of legos, colored markers and paper, a few books, some crackers and fruit. I told him he might need to wait for us in the waiting room where there would be a TV and some other toys and he could draw or play and would have to be patient and wait. He seemed agreeable and unperturbed. What was all the fuss? This was nothing unusual in Fin's mind.

We met Mary Cay and Manny in the lobby and I showed Fin the room where he would wait for us. I went down the hall to sit with Luella for a few moments. I was not surprised to find her looking angelic, a beautiful lady, even on her death bed. Wispy white hair was combed and arranged on her pillow. She wore a soft, yet crisp, white cotton nightgown. She looked clean and settled and sure of herself, even now. Although she could not respond to my voice, I felt as if she knew we were here to sing for her. And I believe she welcomed us.

Once again, the family had gathered, this time to be with their mother as she left the world. The door to the adjoining room was open as was the door to the outside deck. The children were busy coloring and several games were spread out on the picnic table. There were bowls of grapes and goldfish crackers and pretzels. Fin was welcomed to join the family. I had brought him to the perfect sing.

I retrieved Fin from the waiting room and watched him merge easily with the other kids on the deck as we gathered around Luella's bed. The singing, as it often does, changed the way the room felt. The light grew quieter. Conversations stopped and the family moved closer. Luella became the center of everyone's attention as we sang words to say what the heart felt. Tears flowed naturally and easily. Family life flowed too. Death in this family was a part of life. The rhythm of life did not stop because death had come. The dogs needed water and a walk. A home cooked meal, delivered by the visiting health aides, would be coming in 20 minutes, along with cousins and more friends to say goodbye to Luella. There was sorrow here, but there was life to do. Luella had always understood this.

I noticed Fin, a marker in his fist, peer into the room as we sang. His curious eyes rested on Luella in her bed. And then he was gone, back to the business of children.

On the way home I asked him what he had noticed. "Was that the lady dying?" he asked. "She looked like she was sleeping," he stated. "Yes, that was Luella," I told him. "Sometimes dying looks like going to sleep and sometimes it looks like hard work." "What do you think?" I asked this small bright boy. "Good." he said, and shrugged his shoulders. "Can we get an ice cream?" "Why not," I said. And we did.

Singers Keeping Company

Mike

Sometimes there are no visitors. Sometimes, we visit a person at the end of their life and we look upon loneliness. Sunlight spills through a dirty window. There are flimsy blankets and food trays with a bent straw protruding from juice in a plastic container. Untouched mashed potatoes. A television set stares cold and empty from above. The remote sits on the movable tray beside the bed.

Mike has no family visiting him, we are told. He is alone. He is 50 years old, actively dying. What is his story, we wonder. It doesn't matter. We are here to sing for him, to keep him company in his final hours.

Ellen warms up the singers in the hallway in front of the elevator. We are on the third floor of a local nursing home. I go to sit with Mike for a few quiet moments. There is a nurse's aide sitting quietly beside him when I enter. She smiles and offers me her place in a chair pulled next to the bed. Mike is unresponsive. He is in a state of elsewhere. I sit in silence for a few moments, watching his chest rise and fall. This man is younger than me. He has no family, though he must have, at some point. I watch my wondering mind and then I let it rest. I become still. I fall into rhythm with Mike's breaths and I speak softly to tell him some friends have come to visit and sing. We are grateful to be here with him. I tell him to stay wherever he is and rest in the sounds of our voices.

By the time I return to the others, they have grown more quiet as a group. They are barely moving. Some have closed their eyes. They are humming, making a lovely vibration that seems to fill the dingy hallway with pastel colors. I join the circle, tell them who I met in room 307, and we hum again to flow, as one being, into the room to find our places around Mike's bed. Some stand and others sit as we sing. The songs are prayers. They are voices in conversation with a lonely man at the end of his life. We hum between songs. Though Mike is in a coma, we can feel him respond through subtle changes in his breath, a softening around the mouth, the slightest flutter of eyelids, a possible sigh. A sense of peace has entered the room and has touched each one of us. We sing this peace. We cannot bring ourselves to leave this bedside and so we stay and stay, singing, humming and sitting in silence with Mike.

Paul

Paul had just been released from prison. We didn't know his backstory or how many years he had spent in jail. We didn't know why he had been imprisoned. We knew that he had two people visiting him in his hospital room. One was his parole officer, the other an Episcopalian minister. We knew that he was in rapid decline from lung cancer and had been given a prognosis of weeks, and that he was 63 years old. And we knew that he loved music. Hospice was now involved in his end-of-life care. We were called to sing.

The first sing we scheduled did not come together as planned. It was the last week of February and Paul was being transferred from a rehabilitation center to a hospital for surgery on an incarcerated hernia. Ryan, our hospice coordinator, told Paul that a small group of singers would visit him post-op and that even if he were not awake to know we were there, perhaps our presence would be felt.

We were called again on the 4th of March. I was away visiting family. It seems I was not the only one unavailable to sing that day. Fred tried to get a group together with no luck. Most often, when Hallowell members are invited to a bedside, they will leave work early, change plans, leave the bread half baked and the soup ingredients on the cutting board to get to a sing. But every once in a while, it doesn't work easily to find a balanced group of singers. Such was the case when the call to sing for Paul in his hospital room came through. Fred was moved to make the visit anyway, and so he went to meet Paul on his own. Here is Fred's report from that visit:

A group was not meant to happen today, as it turned out; but nevertheless, I felt called to go over by myself. Paul had just finished lunch, so was still sitting on the edge of his bed, but said that he wasn't really up for any singing. I said that I completely understood, but offered him The Lord's Prayer (in song) before I left. He said that would be nice. So I sang it for him. After I finished, he said he wouldn't mind another, so I sang Celtic Blessing. Then he asked for another (I sang, Now the Day is Over from our blue hymnal), and then another (Gaelic Blessing).

Between each one, we chatted for a minute. He said that he is really looking forward to having "a show" from Hallowell (I let him know that our singing is really anything but!), but that the timing just hadn't been right any of the times that it had been offered. I assured him that it is always fine for the person we sing for to just lie with their eyes closed and listen, but he said he really wanted to be present enough to be able to appreciate it fully. He also said that he was feeling a little better every day, so sometime in the next couple of days sounded like a good time to try again with a group.

After Gaelic Blessing, he said "I think I should call it a day" but then he kept chatting for a few more minutes anyway. We talked about the joy of giving (I had thanked him for letting me stay and sing for him) and how much wonderful music there is in the world.

So it ended up being perfect that I hadn't arrived with a group (I think even a foursome would have been too much), but he really seemed to appreciate the small solo offering that I made.

On the 7th of March, Paul was transferred once more. This time to the hospice room at Grace Cottage Hospital where he would die.

Larry, Tom and I arrived at Grace Cottage as darkness fell. We piled our coats on chairs in the waiting room, and carried only our Hallowell books down the well lit hallway to the room at the end, where we found Paul close to death. Here it was quiet and the lighting was softer. His parole officer and his friend the minister were keeping close vigil. They left the bedside to rest in the adjoining room as we pulled three chairs close to Paul's bedside and began our two hour vigil sing. The loosened yellowed skin of Paul's face had lost all elasticity. It draped over his protruding cheekbones in folds. His breathing was labored and noisy with long hesitations between breaths. His eyes were sunken in their sockets, slightly open, but not seeing, rolled back in his head.

The three of us sat close together, shoulders touching. We sang hymns. We sat in stillness between songs. We hummed. We sang songs in foreign languages that told stories of solace and rest. We watched Paul labor towards his death. The officer and the minister hovered in the doorway between the rooms while we sang, holding a thread to this lonely man's life. We sang him out of the world.

Paul died a few hours after we left his bedside. We carried a piece of him away with us that night, the story we didn't know, the feeling of an untold life. We thought perhaps we had witnessed loneliness and transformation. We were with him as he was dying, and we wanted to be. As did the others who chose to keep vigil and stay beside him as he left the world.

We were all there on the riverbank a week later, Larry, Tom and I along with Paul's parole officer, the minister and Ryan from hospice. The cold March wind invited us to keep our coats buttoned and our hats on. The edges of the river were laced with ice, but there was enough of a current here to watch Paul's ashes float freely downstream as we sang *"I've got peace like a river, I've got peace like a river in my soul."*

We sang and we shed tears. We were the only witnesses to Paul's end of life journey. Each one of us felt loss and hope grow in our own hearts as we said goodbye and watched his remains become one with the flow of the river.

Photo: John Nopper

EIGHT

TEACHERS AND FURTHER STORIES

Each person we sing for, each person dying before us, leaves a story. From each experience, our practice grows in depth and width. The next three stories honor some of our greatest teachers.

Hallowell practices in a small community in Vermont, a place where we often have a personal connection to those we are called to serve. A sensitivity to each situation, personality and family dynamic is called for each time a sing is organized. There are cases where we intentionally form a group of singers who don't know the person in the bed, or the family. This is a way to offer privacy. It relieves the person we are visiting from any feelings of needing to connect or be host to us. There is no expectation of a relationship that could energetically drain a person who is working hard to live until they let go to die. We visit as anonymous, yet loving, strangers.

In Mark's case, however, we did the opposite. For Mark, connection was the medicine that best served him. Each singer invited to visit him had been following his story and shared a friendship and personal connection with him.

Mark's response to terminal brain cancer was to write a blog and to publicly invite people to be with him on his journey. His home and his story were open to others. He welcomed questions and conversations about his cancer.

Mark was a teacher of life. He lived fully until he died.

Tom and Sue taught us about generosity and allowed us a glimpse into the life of a couple who were devoted to each other. We learned a new language of heart and listening by watching their relationship as they had to let each other go through death.

And Jeff was the master of equanimity. Jeff and Genie opened their home and hearts to friends and family and invited others to share the experience of Jeff's death. It is a rare thing in our culture to witness a good death. Jeff's acceptance of, and reverence for, his final days, offered a lasting gift and a truth about what's possible at the end of a life well lived.

To each person who has invited us to stand in their presence and be with them for a small part of their journey of dying, we are respectfully grateful and realize that each one is a teacher of the highest regard. Through their invitation to sing at the bedside and stand close to their process, the cultural practices of death and dying are changing. We are remembering to celebrate life and to accept death. We are remembering that we can be with our loved ones as they die and we can help to create a journey that aides the dying through their process and strengthens and comforts those left behind.

Stories

❧

The World Grows Quiet

The first time I met Mark was in the admissions office at The Putney School when my wildly creative son Jason was applying and being interviewed as a potential student. There was Mark behind his grin and his glasses, a bright, humorous, easy going man, who made my nervous son feel like he was worth every bit as much as the next guy and more. He put him at ease. He made Jason believe that he, Mark, was truly excited about having him at this school, that the school was a special place, and that creative students like Jason were the very reason why.

I saw Mark again at family court one gray day when we were being instructed by a mediator about how to file for divorce without an attorney. We made light of it, understating the irony of how many of us knew each other in the courtroom that day. And yet, there was something about sharing such an experience that bound us together in a place of change and acceptance. We watched our families unravel and untangle, as we learned how to parent our children with our soon-to-be exes, beyond our marriages.

Last spring, while Mark was still able-bodied enough to get around and be out and about, I ran into him two hours north of our home town on Church Street at an outdoor restaurant. Every chance encounter with this big hearted man was met with gladness, hugs and conversation that mattered. This time it was about his health, the brain cancer that had pulled the rug out from under his good life, the way the sun felt warm that spring day, the way people were out in droves on a fine April afternoon in Vermont. I watched him limp away, leaning into his friend as they walked, shoulder to shoulder on the uneven cobblestones, a wool hat on his bald head, his glasses askew. I noticed how he had grown thinner and smaller, as if he were starting to disappear. Mark. How much longer would he be in this world?

When the left side of his body gave up on him, when hospice was called in to help make him comfortable at home, when the community rallied to raise money for a full time, at-home-caretaker to be with him, Hallowell was called to go and sing for Mark.

He waited for us in his wheelchair. A wool blanket covered his lap and the tubing that had become part of his body. A hat covered his head. He wore wire rimmed glasses that reflected the light from the laptop opened on the desk in front of him. He greeted each of us and thanked us before we even started for coming to sing for him.

After a settling in time, we set the tone with "Plovi Barko," melodic, soothing tones from the Dalmatian coast of Croatia. We sang, "Crossing the Bar." Mark moved between tears and open weeping to singing along. He soaked in the songs, one after another. Some brought light conversation afterward. Others brought fresh tears. "Blessed Quietness" invited quiet. The quiet grew in all of us.

We were not somber, just respectfully reverent for where we were, who we were with and what we were doing, singing around our friend Mark.

When it was clearly time for a last song, I needed a moment of silence to find it. We wanted to leave Mark with the song that said what our hearts wanted to say or what his heart wanted to hear. Our silence was full of respect and question. It was not awkward. Finally, the song came with clarity. "Fear Not the Pain" would be our last song. This was a song recently added to our repertoire, a few lines of a Rilke poem that had been put to music and could be sung like a chant.

I stood behind Mark with my hands on his shoulders. Mark's caretaker, a lovely young woman, stood facing me across the room and nodded in approval. Val sat across from Mark. She closed her eyes. Halfway through the song, she opened her eyes and reached for Mark's hand. Singers Mark G and Tom stood solidly and steadily nearby. Leslie and Kathy M were quietly present. I told Mark this song was part of a larger poem and that he could find it easily on the internet, which he did. I asked him if he would like me to read it between our singing. He said yes. Please. He closed his eyes and bowed his head as if in prayer. Tears continually leaked out of the corners of his eyes and fell quietly onto his wool blanket.

We sang, *"Fear not the pain. Let its weight fall back into the earth. For heavy are the mountains. Heavy are the seas."*

I read:

You who let yourselves feel: enter the breathing

that is more than your own.
Let it brush your cheeks
as it divides and rejoins behind you.

We sang:
*"Fear not the pain. Let its weight fall back into the earth. For heavy
are the mountains. Heavy are the seas."*

Blessed ones, whole ones,
you where the heart begins:
You are the bow that shoots the arrows
and you are the target.

*"Fear not the pain. Let its weight fall back into the earth. For heavy
are the mountains. Heavy are the seas."*

Fear not the pain. Let its weight fall back
into the earth;
for heavy are the mountains, heavy the seas.

*"Fear not the pain. Let its weight fall back into the earth. For heavy
are the mountains. Heavy are the seas."*

The trees you planted in childhood have grown
too heavy. You cannot bring them along.
Give yourselves to the air, to what you cannot hold.

*"Fear not the pain. Let its weight fall back into the earth. For heavy
are the mountains. Heavy are the seas."*

We left Mark in a state of grace. We left in a state of grace.
We each said a gentle goodbye to him. This was not the kind of
departure from a sing where we slip out quietly humming, leaving
as seamlessly as possible. Mark needed us to each have a moment of
closure and gratitude with him. I slid his hat back and pressed my
lips against his soft bald head. He pulled me into a hug and held on
with a strength that surprised me.

I saw Mark next, in his home in Walpole, for a second visit
and sing. This time, we found him in his recliner. Visits evolve.
Each subsequent sing takes a new shape and form. We never know
what to expect when we walk through the doorway into someone's
home or room where change is occurring.

Inside the space where someone is dying, a kind of time warp
takes place. We forget how long we've been there. We forget where
we just came from or where we will be going next. We are simply
there, in that place of transformation where a spirit is working hard
to leave the physical body, and change is happening right before our
eyes, though we may not see it.

We had heard that Mark was growing more tired and distant.
He was crying easily and often. We had learned from hospice that he
was in decline, nearing the end of his life.

We ventured out into the fast falling snow as darkness
descended. The roads were slippery. Branches, outlined in white,
displayed the shapes of trees along the back roads. The winter world
grew quiet.

We made tracks to Mark's house, tracks to his door. We tried
to take off our boots and snow-filled coats as quietly as possible

without falling over each other in the tiny entryway, humming all the while as we eased our way in. I had already been in ahead of the others to connect with Mark. He was resting in his leather recliner, wrapped in blankets. I told him we were not here to be social and so he should feel free to sleep or keep his eyes closed while we sang. He was grateful for this offer.

We sang over and around him. Tears slipped down his face. There was no full-out sobbing this time. These tears felt calm and accepting. Mark whispered "thanks" and "beautiful" after every song.

The songs tonight felt like prayers. Mark seemed to absorb and receive every word. We sang "Sing to Me of Heaven." *There will be no sorrow there, in heaven above where all is love, there'll be no sorrow there.* We sang, "Love Call Me Home." *When I cry in my sleep, friends carry me over. When I'm weary and cannot swim, love call me home. Time ferry me down the river, friends carry me safely over, life tend me on my journey, love call me home.*

Five friends stood and sat around Mark, grateful to be able to sing words we were unable to say. We sang of blessed quietness and the farthest field full of beauty. We sang about angels hovering around, about journeys and about love. This time we hummed our way back out into the stormy snowy evening and left Mark in a veil of quiet and rest.

Inside that home something mysterious occurred. A change so profound and wondrous, we could not name it. A man we called friend, a man we called Mark, was dying. That evening he was among us, resting in his nest of blankets, counting the days he had

left, counting his breaths. Soon he would be gone. The chair empty.
The body lifeless. The spirit away.

    We circled while the snow covered our heads and shoulders
and the cold wind pushed against us. We absorbed the love we had
felt being with our friend, the warmth in our hearts enough to keep
us warm inside of our circle.

Quiet
for Mark

Winter has brought us to our knees again.
We are asking to remember green,
praying for faith to believe that beneath this cover of snow
lie the gardens we so carefully tended once
the bulbs we planted with hope in our hands.

On our winter knees, heads bowed,
we wonder what the sun feels like
warm on the upturned face.
We remember open windows, open fields.

I'm up to my knees in it,
that softest blanket of snow
that fell in the night.
I lift my snowshoes, one step at a time
muscles working, breath.
I make paths; to the compost,
to the bees, to the trails through woods.

The world narrows in winter,
becomes roads and driveways,
paths that lead to uncertainty.

I know a man whose world has narrowed this winter.
His has become the inside walls of his old farm house,
the arms of his soft recliner in the still-living room,
the edges of his bed.
He watches winter through the window,
wool cap on his bald head,
fleece blanket over his lap, hands tucked in.
He searches for the words to say,
"It's so quiet." about the falling snow.

The bulbs will push through the black earth again.
Color will be restored to our eyes and hearts.
Birds will sing from budding treetops,
bring sweet songs to warming days.
Hope will spring again.

But in this one old farm house, a recliner will rest empty
where this man I knew had been brought to his knees,
where he asked only for the quiet he saw outside his window
as the snow fell,
and went there.

Devotion

Sue sat at her round dining table, the chair pulled aside so her wheel-chair could fit into place. On the table in front of her was a vessel, covered by a knitted prayer shawl. She leaned against it with her forehead, eyes closed. Her breathing was soft and even as if she were merging with the ashes contained inside. There was a quiet around her. The quiet of candle light. The quiet of reverence. The quiet of grief.

It was a bitter winter evening, below zero temperatures. The ground was frozen solid, with patches of ice and snow that called us to watch our footing as we made our way into the softly lit folds of this familiar house. We had been coming here to sing for over a year.

The first call from hospice to come to this house was planned as a visit and sing for Sue, who had suffered a stroke. She had trouble communicating due to some aphasia, but she managed. Though she lived with her husband Tom, who remained close beside her in daily life, a full time caretaker had been hired to live with them. Tom could not provide the kind of care assistance Sue needed now.

I knocked on the strong wooden door of this old-barn-converted-to-beautiful-home. Tom answered the door with a warm welcome, his kind face and gentle manner put everyone instantly at ease. While I went in ahead to connect with Sue, the other singers took off their coats and boots and waited in the expansive entryway, feeling the sense of place here. Sometimes the rightness of a place enters you immediately. It speaks of a life well lived and tended. The land is tended. The home is tended. The heart is tended. There is a moment, when you enter a stranger's home, when they are no longer a stranger because you recognize their way of living and feel welcoming presences. This was true of Tom and Sue's home. You could almost feel the pulse of years of friends and family within the walls. You could almost read the stories of their lives by looking at the artwork on the walls, clay bowls full of fruit, pottery on open shelves, warm tiles in the kitchen and open spaces framed by timbers and wide spans of windows where light flooded in and your view swept out across the expanse of meadow. Books with familiar titles, classics and poetry, lined shelves. Framed photographs of people we recognized from the community rested on tables. Sue was propped in her chair in the sun, looking small and expectant and glad to have us come to sing for her.

Tom pulled his chair beside her. Just before he settled in, he had a short coughing fit. His cough led me to ask after his health. We learned that he had just had his second round of chemotherapy that morning and that he was a bit tired. We realized that we were here to sing for both Sue and Tom, each on their own journey, separately and together.

Tom and Sue listened intently and applauded after we finished our first song. We suggested they relax, receive and allow. We were not here to perform, just sing. When I realized it might be a bit of a challenge for them to be comfortable with the attention, we brought in chairs and sat on the sofa. We became part of the living room feeling, rather than standing above them where they sat. They moved closer together then. Tom reached over and took Sue's hand. She closed her eyes. The song "All Through the Night" invited her to open her eyes and smile. She sang along, every word to every verse. We sang and they received with grace and gratitude, for almost an hour. After our tenth song, we signaled to each other to hum our way out so that Tom and Sue might remain in their closeness for a while longer without disruption. We closed the door between the mudroom and the house, leaving them in light and privacy. We pulled on our boots and coats, still humming, and slipped out into the yard where we formed our closing circle. We reached our arms across each other's shoulders, breathed together, checked in verbally, and shared some moments that had touched or taught us.

Before we departed to return to our daily lives, I went back into the house to give Tom and Sue copies of our two CD's. I found them still sitting side by side, still holding onto each other's hand. This would be the last time over the coming year that Tom would let us see ourselves out. But we were glad that for at least this time, they gave themselves the gift of settling into the songs and staying with the tenderness it had brought them for a while longer.

We visited Sue and Tom's place many times over the next year. In mud-season we drove up the hill piled into two 4-wheel drive trucks. In summer, the view out the south windows took our breath away, inspiring us to sing "Farthest Field." "We don't know that one," Tom told us after the last note. "It's not on your CD." They had listened every day since our initial visit to both of our record-ings, learning every song and singing along with us during sings. They had favorites they would ask for. And we would try to sing a few new ones to add to the repertoire. Tom and Sue learned to relax in the songs, to receive the music without feeling the need to clap for us. They would sing. They would sigh. They would share small stories or pieces of history from their life together. Always, they sat side by side in the sun, holding hands.

Over time, we realized that it gave Tom great pleasure to welcome us in and walk us to the door to say goodbye. He was a man with a generous heart. He would offer us lunch. Tea. Drinks. Towards the end of summer, as we were leaving a sing, Tom said, "I really want to have you over for hors d'oeuvres and martinis." We laughed of course and said, "Well, we would have to make that a non-Hallowell social call. But it sounds like fun." He looked so sincere.

It seemed important to him somehow, to be able to give something to us in return for our visits and singing. No matter how much we tried to explain that every time we were invited to come and sing for them, we were gifted by the way they enjoyed and received our songs, there was something more Tom needed to do. It was the generous host in him. "We will consider it and try to find a time," we said as we were leaving that day. That time didn't come until after Tom died.

The next time we visited, in early fall, the caretaker greeted us at the door. We found Tom and Sue in the same corner of the room, flooded in the last light of day, holding hands, quietly waiting for our arrival. Tom looked grey, tired and shrunken. Still he was gracious and welcomed us from where he sat beside Sue.

This visit would be the last time we would sing for Tom. His health took a turn for the worse and he died a week later. The news saddened us. We had grown so fond of him, so moved by his devotion to Sue and their apparent love for each other. Tom had taught us how it is as much an act of generosity to accept an offer of kindness as to give one.

Two days after we got news of Tom's death, I received the following email from Sue's visiting hospice nurse:

I write with significant news. Tom M. passed away last night. He died peacefully and he was surrounded by his family.

I met with Sue today. She said she would like you all to come and sing as soon as possible. We wondered together if Thursday around the cocktail hour would work for you? It's short notice. Another day would work too, preferably around the cocktail hour and here's why.

Tom and Sue had a plan that the Hallowell singers would come and sing and then have cocktails and hors d'oeuvres on the house. Sue would like to complete this plan if possible.

You could call the caretaker at the house tomorrow and make the arrangements with her. If you wouldn't mind confirming your receipt of this message that would be great. Also, please call or write if you have any questions.

Thanks so much for all your beautiful music and comforting and healing presence. It means so much to so many!

We agreed. How else could we respond to such an unusual and wonderful invitation. We understood that this would be a way to honor Tom by finally accepting his generous offer of hospitality. I called the caretaker to arrange a time for our visit, making it clear that we would be honored to come and sing for Sue as soon as possible and that it was not necessary to have food and drinks, but that if it felt somehow important to share that with us, if it would offer closure and connection, we would accept this lovely invitation graciously and with gratitude.

Our group of seven gathered in the driveway to sing through a song as a way to feel bonded before we moved together into this home full of fresh grief. Daughter Sarah and son Tony were both there to welcome us. Sue, a shawl over her shoulders, was in her wheelchair, pulled into the round dining table. On the mantle behind her, an altar of photographs, flowers and beeswax candles had been beautifully arranged in remembrance of Tom. Light was filling their home.

Sue seemed to receive our singing in her very soul. When we sang the familiar ones, she closed her eyes and sang along. When we sang a new one, she closed her eyes and listened to the words and feeling of the song. When we offered a song for Tom and sang "May You See Diamonds" for the first time in this home, Sue received it in just this way. And when we sang the lyrics—*May you hear angels in the darkness of the night. And may you sing among us, through every earthly choir*—we all thought we could almost sense Tom's presence standing with us, singing.

After a few songs, Sue began to cry softly and speak of Tom. "Why did he have to die first?" she asked through soft sobs. "I was supposed to go first. Why am I still here? He held my hand every night," she said. Sarah came close to her mother then and held her shoulders from behind. Tony moved his chair closer too, and took her hand. The moment invited us to move nearer to Sue too. We became a smaller, tighter circle of support, of love, of songs spilling from our hearts one after another. We responded with a quiet version of "Angels Hovering Round."

This may have been the first time we have sung to someone in their home just days after a loved one has died. What do we know of the timing of things? Of life and death? It was a poignant and deeply moving experience to be here in this powerful moment of grief and closeness with this family.

We sang for a long and gentle time. There was no awkwardness about the social time after the official sing-part was over. Tony and Sarah made us lovely light martinis with ice and olives. On the kitchen counter was a beautiful spread of cheeses and salami, olives and crackers and thin slices of pear and apple. We surrounded Sue, lifted our glasses in a toast to Tom and understood the truth about what it means to be truly generous.

Stories from the family morphed into singing rounds from their childhood, sung in the car on the way from New York to Vermont. We knew many of the rounds and joined them in singing their old favorites. Tears and laughter flowed to ease the weight of grief. Much to our delight, Sue and her daughter Sarah sang some old Japanese songs Sue had taught her children when they were young. Tony just laughed. We were careful not to overstay our welcome and ended the evening by singing the round *Onawa's Waltz* and seeing ourselves out....or at least trying to. We were followed by both Sarah and Tony, who thanked us as we thanked them.

"It just keeps growing" Larry said as we held each other, almost speechless, in our closing circle. We all knew exactly what he meant.

We sang at Tom's memorial service the day before Thanksgiving. And we continued to visit and sing for Sue regularly until she died. The evening we found her holding Tom's ashes, keeping him warm with the prayer shawl, was the last time she would sing along with us or ask for a certain song or cry softly while we sang around her in a loving circle. She held onto that vessel while we sang. She lifted her head up once or twice to beam at us, but would return to Tom, his remains, his memory. Her longing and grief were palpable. Her attentive caretaker sat close beside her, watching her and waiting to be of service. She offered tissues. She stayed tuned in. Sue wiped quiet tears. Sometimes I noticed her mouth moving to a song she knew and loved. Sometimes the songs fall like prayers onto the person listening, into the open heart. The songs that evening were those kind of prayers—they said words that were heard and felt. Sue was quiet and private, receptive and devoted. Always devoted to her beloved Tom.

We eased our way out of the warm softly lit house back into the frozen January night. We hummed our way into the dark, into our closing circle, where we bowed our heads together and touched foreheads, merging, integrating, honoring and bowing to all we are so privileged to witness.

The last call to the home of Tom and Sue came at 4:30 in the afternoon in late January. Sue had suffered another stroke. She was in bed now and unresponsive. Her daughter Sarah had arrived.

Tony and another daughter were on their way. Could we come as soon as possible?

We managed to gather a group of singers quickly. We found Mary Cay on her way home from Greenfield and intercepted Mark between work and rehearsal. Tom and I left our warm home and once again ventured out into the icy winds of late January.

The four of us gathered around Sue in her bed, small and lost in the folds of her comforter. Her daughter sat beside her while her first born granddaughter listened on the held phone while we sang. Two beloved caretakers had come to say goodbye. Some friends had gathered. There was a feel of family, life, home, death. All just right. All part of the flow of a life well lived, a family well loved, a home well tended. Sue would leave this world the next day, after her two other children arrived in time to be with her as she died. We sang songs in other languages that night. Songs that would not call her back from wherever she might be. We could only hope our sounds and songs helped her to let go, to go to a place where she might find Tom waiting to take her hand again.

Equanimity

A small girl perched on a stone, knees bent, bare feet on solid rock. Her arms wrapped around her legs and her chin rested on her knees. Strands of silky hair lifted in the summer breeze. She raised her head when we drove in and leapt off the rock to greet us, as if she had been waiting for us all day. She told me her name was Violet. "Of course," I said. "I *thought* you were a fairy." Her eyes shone like jewels in the sun. She was a fairy, eight-year-old Violet, and she grabbed my hand as if she had known me forever, to lead me into her grandparents' home. Ten-year-old Oliver, a bit more serious than his fairy sister, waited at the door to escort me. I gladly let myself be guided into this welcoming home by the children to go and meet Jeff, whom we had been told, we would fall in love with.

The other five singers warmed up voices and hearts amidst the row of shade trees outside. The land here was cared for by knowing hands. Mowed paths passed through blooming perennial gardens to wood-sided outbuildings. Strong stone walls led to the pond, where another young grandchild splashed in the clear water, under the attending eyes of a babysitter. We were enchanted by the beauty of this place.

Violet pulled me into the kitchen to meet her grandmother "Poppy," aka Genie, who was busy pulling blueberry scones out of the oven. Genie brushed flour off of her hands onto her apron and pulled me into a full embrace. Genie was like that, I would come to realize, a flower of a woman. The kind of woman who makes you remember your most beloved grandmother. The kind of woman you feel drawn to spend time with, to talk, eat, to laugh or cry. Open-hearted and true.

Violet's mother, Comfort, was also in the kitchen. We talked as if we were old friends. The welcoming kitchen, smell of scones, the familiar mother-daughter-granddaughter ease invited us to talk lightly. We spoke of grandchildren, of fairies and summer camps. Somehow, in the midst of our seemingly light-hearted conversation, it was communicated to me that Comfort and her family lived in Newtown, Connecticut, and that these young children had recently lived through a trauma no child should ever have to witness. I tucked that piece of news into my heart where the children had already found a place. Then I went to meet Jeff.

He was resting comfortably in a sunlit corner of the living room. High ceilings and wooden beams framed bright open spaces in this house. Wall hangings, sculptures and paintings by local artists warmed the room as did the comfortable chairs and couches in woven fabrics. Genie had placed snacks and glasses for iced tea on a long oak table, an arrangement of fresh flowers at the center.

The room was full of light. Jeff's eyes were too. He immediately took both of my hands in his and with a strong yet tender grip told me how grateful he was that we had come to sing. He was resting and waiting now, he told me. "I am at the end of my life," Jeff said, "and these past weeks have been some of the best I've ever known." Jeff was diagnosed with a rare, aggressive and difficult to treat non-Hodgkin's Mantle Cell Lymphoma. In the last months of Jeff's life, a ground breaking treatment was discovered which proved to be helpful to about 85% of those afflicted with the disease. Unfortunately, Jeff was not one of them. He was home now, here to live out his final days among family, friends and beauty. He felt like a holy man to me.

His smile was effortless. He emanated kindness. Gentleness. Acceptance. Wonder. Equanimity, I thought. When all things— hard and soft, dark or light, joyful or sorrowful—remain in balance in your spirit. When you look through an inclusive lens and see the whole story. Birth, life, death and the tapestry that weaves it together, an intricate design of truth. Jeff held that up for us to see as we made a small group of ourselves and lit up the room and everyone's faces with our songs.

Our voices, in harmony, were notes leaning against other notes, rich bass tones against tenor against alto spiraling through the soprano melody. Something settled as soon as we began to sing.

Listeners and singers grew quiet in body, mind, and spirit. We call it presence, being present and calling others into presence. There were no performers and no audience. We were joined in the spirit of the song. We anointed with music those listening with their hearts, bearing witness to their story of death in the room, to loss, grief, and their love. It all showed up more fully when we started to sing. We welcomed tears, of joy or sorrow.

We sang "I Still Have Joy" to smiles and nods of agreement and a few wiped away tears. Jeff had spent time with each grandchild, answering their questions about his impending death. He shared his experience, reassuring them that though he was sad to say goodbye to those he loved, he was not afraid. Healing comes in unexpected ways. The faces of these three children were glowing and wide open with smiles while we sang.

We moved easily from song to song, this group so confidant musically and soulfully allowed me as leader the space to listen without distraction, to "read the room," to know intuitively what to sing next, what to say through spoken words or songs, how to be with this family. Between the first few songs, Jeff shared stories. And then, at a tender moment, we sang the one that would bring Genie, in tears, to Jeff's bedside, to take his hand and bury her face in his chest to cry and hold and love. *Let the life I've lived speak for me. When I've come to the end of this road, and I lay down my heavy load, let the life I've lived, speak for me. Let the friends I've made, work I've done, love I've shared—speak for me.*

This is the one they would ask for again. This simple song is the one that broke them open. This is the one we would sing at Jeff's memorial service, because he asked us to. It was exactly what he wanted to say to the world he loved as he was leaving it; Remember the way I lived, worked and loved. Isn't that what each of us would want at the end of our life?

When we sang "Over the Rainbow," Violet came to stand with us, my arm rested on her shoulder. She sang for her grandparents. And then Oliver, to everyone's surprise, asked if we knew "Amazing Grace" and if he could sing it with us. If there had been any dry eyes before this, there weren't now. I couldn't help but wonder how many times these children had sung that song over the past months at the memorial services of their peers. Children just like them victims of a shooting. And now grandfather Jeff was here to tell them that dying could be a beautiful experience. We were all here to witness and to sing to that shimmering notion.

We sang "Angels Hovering Round" to close our time here. Genie, smiling widely, pointed up above our heads where two angel sculptures were suspended from the high ceiling. Suddenly this song that we have been singing for twelve years took on yet another story and deepened itself in our hearts and voices. Angels were hovering indeed.

It was most unusual for us to be called back a day later. Genie called to say how much they loved our visit, how happy it made all of them. She seemed to understand that what we offer through song is a true service of the heart. When Genie called it was to ask if we could return the following Wednesday, when cousins would be visiting to say goodbye to Jeff. We would be honored, I told her, because it was true.

When we returned, it was another group of singers who gathered, this time with Valerie leading musically as I "held the space" as we say, meaning I represented the whole group by being the front relational person. In this family, however, Jeff had a deep curiosity about everyone who stepped over the threshold. He was still looking for connections just days before he died. "Who are you? What do you do? Where do you live?" He tried to know each one of us, though we worked to keep it to a minimum to preserve what little strength he had left.

We found Jeff changed already, in just four days. His skin tone had darkened to a shade of yellowish gray. He seemed shrunken, more exhausted. And yet, as soon as we shaped ourselves, humming around him, he opened his eyes and smiled. His eyes held light, a kind of looking-beyond-this-world sight.

We never got back to sing for Jeff again. He died a few days after our second visit. He left very clear instructions about his memorial service for his family, which included having Hallowell sing. "Let the Life I've Lived Speak for Me" and "I Still Have Joy" were two of Jeff's requested songs. We stood before a room of hundreds of people mourning their beloved friend and colleague and sang the words he wanted them to hear. *Let the love I've shared, speak for me. When I come to the end of this road, and I lay down my heavy load, let the love I've shared, speak for me.* There was no denying that the life this man had lived and the way he chose to die spoke clearly for him. He was a teacher for us all.

NINE

THE SONGS WE SING

One might wonder how we keep from growing tired of singing the same songs. Our Hallowell books are full of the songs we have gathered over more than a decade. Some have been sung hundreds of times, over and over, at bedsides, in lobbies, on stages, during rehearsals and workshops and in the recording studio. They don't lose what they carry. We don't grow tired of singing the same old songs. In fact, they grow over time, with the fullness of the stories they collect. They gain momentum as they travel with us and bestow new listening hearts each time. These songs anoint. They bless. They offer themselves as prayers among the dying and their grieving family. Each time an old song is shared, it is heard by someone for the first time. In that way it stays fresh and energized. And each time a song becomes part of someone's story, their story becomes part of that song.

Occasionally someone at a sing will request a song. The song does not live in our book. We have not rehearsed it. Some of us may not even know the song. If someone requests a specific song, we will attempt to sing it and add harmony if it feels natural to do so. Larry has sung, solo, "Old Man River" in his rich bass voice while the rest of us joined in oooo's or humming behind him and joined him on the chorus. He has done the same with "Danny Boy" or other requested hymns. I have referred to Larry as Hallowell's "walking hymnal." He has a file of old hymns in his head, which come in handy when someone requests one that isn't in the "Little Blue Hymnal" we all keep tucked into the back of our books, a collection of frequently asked-for-hymns that Ellen put together for Hallowell years ago. "In the Garden" and "How Great Thou Art" and "Precious Lord" have been sung at many bedsides, bringing solace and peace to those who have a relationship with these old hymns. We will, on occasion, sight-read through some of these hymns during rehearsal, but for the most part, we sing them as requested, sight-reading, singing melody or adding harmony as we can.

Stories

Our Songs Grow Wings

As we've done each November for the past years, we gather to sing at the altar for the annual Day of the Dead celebration Brattleboro Hospice offers the community. In downtown Brattleboro, in the thrift shop that funds our local hospice, singers and listeners stand among the racks of clothes and second hand housewares and face the altar, created that day. The altar is filled with images and art, photographs, burning candles and mementos people bring to honor loved ones who have died. The glowing orange light softens our faces as we sing "I'll Fly Away." The thrift shop has been transformed into a temple. As we sing, Chris, sitting on the floor beside her lifetime partner Carol, wipes at her eyes. We sing the final chorus, *When I die, hallelujah by and by, I'll fly away.* With a sense of urgency, she stands up as the last note ends and says, "I have to tell you this story!"

As her mother was dying, Chris played Hallowell's songs for her and sang along with "I'll Fly Away." "When she finally did pass," Chris says, "I remember that I even said to her, 'Fly away mom, fly away.'"

When I ask Chris for permission to use her story in this book, she adds even more to it:

Afterwards, my siblings and I dealt with all the details... cleaned out her room at Valley Cares, made the arrangements for her burial alongside my father and brother, planned for her memorial... and then my sister and brother left. Carol was still away in Macedonia with MC Brass, and so after weeks of vigilance, doctors, details, etc... everything was finally done, and I was alone.

I was sitting on the porch that first morning alone, when I noticed the cardinal. (My mother, FYI, was not a lover of cardinals particularly, but loved the sound of birds in general.) Over the next month or so, a cardinal appeared almost daily, singing, it seemed, just for me. And on my birthday a few weeks later, she actually flew in circles around me, stopping on branch to branch close by, and serenaded me.

Since then, now three years later, on the anniversary of certain events, or poignant moments in my life or with my family, I find that a cardinal shows up somewhere in the day. And I still see it as the presence of my mother, letting me know she's still with us.

So please do tell this story. I truly believe the world is imbued with meaning and significance, and it is only our skeptical, overly rational minds that get in the way of receiving the signs of connection to other realms of reality. And then we miss the blessing they are meant to bring us.

Chris' story entered "I'll Fly Away" that Day of the Dead. Now, when we sing it, there is a cardinal and a mother's love that tells its story through the same old verses.

Hundreds of stories live in between the lines of "How Could Anyone Ever Tell You." The same is true for "Love Call me Home" and "I Still Have Joy." Songs we have been singing from the inception of Hallowell continue to get better. We learn them by heart. I referred to By-Hearting when describing a Hallowell rehearsal in an earlier chapter. Each month, no matter how long we have been singing a song, we choose a By-Heart song. This simply means we spend extra time practicing it so that we know it in the cells of our body. We know these songs so well, we have no need to look at the music. But we look anyway.

During a sing, we bring our books into the room. We give ourselves complete permission to open to the page of the chosen song in case we suddenly need to grab a word or a note. Having our books with us gives us confidence and this in turn keeps us present. Having our books allows the song chooser to scan the table of contents as a song is ending so she might see the next song. It seems to jump out at me when I am in that role. I run my eyes down the list and the next song becomes clear. I have already noticed how the family is responding. I have heard what the daughter said to her mother. I have watched the bowed head, the hand held, the way the son moved closer to his father's bed. I have noticed the breath of the dying person slow down, the lines around the mouth soften, the eyes flutter. I choose the next thing we want to say through song. Choosing songs at the bedside becomes a learned skill. As intuition grows, so does the art of knowing how to respond to the emotions of the moment through the chosen song. There is no wrong song. There are only more right ones.

Choosing songs requires stillness of mind and heart and listening from the core of one's being. The leader is in a state of alertness and awareness. She is reading the room. She is the only one choosing songs. She is watching for responses, subtle or obvious, from the dying person, the family, the singers. She is listening from the far reaching corners of her consciousness, from her inner ear. She is wide open, receptive, kind and compassionate. This is the practice, the art of bedside singing. Each person in the room practices this every time they are present. Sometimes, silence is necessary in order to make a space for this kind of listening. The singers practice being comfortable with silence, with not needing to fill it, but to patiently wait within the walls of silence. The next song will find us if we give it time and trust.

We are also grateful for the way new songs become part of our repertoire and find a place in our book. Peter arranges music with his finely tuned ear. Mary Cay has collected a treasure trove of music from foreign lands, giving us the sounds we need without the familiar language to pull people out of where they are on their unknown-to-us journey. Together, these two music directors keep Hallowell's voice strong and clear. They teach us new music and they revisit the old. They realize the importance of bringing a pure and beautiful sound to the deathbed. The gift we bring is our music. Because of this, it is an essential part of our practice to keep working on our songs, tuning, singing on pitch, listening to and blending with each other, so that each small group can offer the most lovely sound possible.

Here is what Peter Amidon, one of Hallowell's two music directors, has to say about his role:

> My career as a choral leader/arranger/composer has grown mostly in the second half of my life. Hospice singing has enriched and deepened my choral life and career in surprising ways. It has been deeply satisfying to see Mary Alice's (my wife and music partner) choral arrangements and compositions become an important part of the repertoire for hospice singing groups in Vermont and beyond. Co-leading Hallowell has been beyond pleasure. I am inspired by Mary Cay's song contributions and I always learn from her music leadership. Kathy provides the root understanding and the spiritual foundation of everything we do. The multitude of hospice singing groups that have formed since Hallowell started is extraordinary. I feel a creative tension between celebrating the spread of hospice singing, and a concern (almost a responsibility, since Hallowell was the inspiration for most of the a cappella SATB—Soprano, Alto, Tenor, Bass—hospice singing groups of the last twelve years) that the singing in these groups is tuneful and beautiful.

Beyond the Book—Two Stories

What Will Be Will Be

Years ago, we sang for a couple married for fifty years as they celebrated their last anniversary. Arlene would be dead two weeks later. We sat in the living room of their double-wide mobile home. Filtered sun touched the faded arms of the dusty couch where they sat close together, holding each other's hands. When they asked us to sing "Que Sera Sera", we searched each other's faces, wondering, and were pleasantly surprised when Harriet stepped forward and sang every verse, clearly and beautifully while we all joined on the chorus. *Que sera sera, whatever will be, will be. The future's not ours to see, que sera sera.* Although we didn't find it among the pages of our Hallowell book, there could not have been a more perfect song for that moment.

You Are My Sunshine

It is late Friday evening. I arrive home after a full day. A message on my answering machine from hospice says the 91 year old man we sang for in his home last week has died. The next message is from his daughter. Can we sing tomorrow at 11:00 AM for his memorial service?

I rework my Saturday schedule. I cancel and change plans and call everyone who had been at the sing at Carl's home last week. Once again I am amazed and delighted at the intention and commitment of these singers. Every part is covered.

The day we sang for Carl six singers drove up a long dirt road that led to a small house at the top of the hill. Carl and his wife Rose sat side by side in two worn comfortable recliners, a folding table beside each one held tea cups and tissue boxes, a TV remote, ordinary things. Their small but extremely vocal devoted dog took turns jumping from lap to lap to protect "mother" or "father" when we would get too close. Carl wore his flannel shirt unbuttoned at the collar, untucked, over a pair of worn khaki pants. He pointed to the walker beside his chair and explained that he used to love to walk back before he had hip surgery. Now he has to use this walker and take one slow step at a time.

Rose sat beside him, her soft white hair framing her sweet-ly smiling face. Two daughters and a son-in-law brought in chairs from the adjoining dining room and found their places. We sang, "I Still Have Joy," "I Will Guide Thee," "What a Wonderful World," and "Heart of my Heart." After about a half hour of singing, one daughter, Carol, shyly asked if we could possibly sing "You Are My Sunshine." We broke into four part harmony and managed the verses. Carl began to cry. Not trying to stop the flow of tears, he looked toward Rose who reached for his hand across the space between their recliners. They held on tightly. The daughters and son-in-law did not resist their own tears. They later explained to us that Carl had courted Rose with that song seventy-one years ago. He would play it on his guitar and sing to her. We could feel the thread of history and love that wove this family together. All hearts were open, ours included.

After the songs, we were invited into the well worn kitchen where a heaping plate of chocolate chip cookies had just been baked and fresh coffee simmered in a drip pot. As we said our farewell, Rose and Carl's fierce protector set up a barking frenzy that prevented us from getting too close to his people in their recliners. We laughed and settled for waves as we closed the door gently behind us.

There was no way I would have turned down the request to sing at the service just a few days later. It was a service at a funeral home in town. The pastor hadn't known Carl at all and provided a service about Christ and his good works instead of about the grace of Carl's life. The saving grace at the service was Carol reading a piece about her father and our singing of "Amazing Grace" and, of course, "You Are My Sunshine."

Rose sat quietly in the front row among her three daughters, her dog on her lap. I went to her gently, after our singing ended the service, to hug her. The dog remained perfectly still and quiet.

Carl's love for Rose and his family could be felt in the rays of sunshine that sang through us that day and entered the grieving hearts of family. There is a place for every song, whether it comes from the pages of our book or directly from the heart of a family story remembered through the verses of a favorite song.

Thuma Mina

Betsy is one hundred and four years old when death comes to her. We are called to her bedside on a warm spring day. Betsy's daughter, her caretaker Lea and I sit quietly together in Betsy's room at the residential care facility where she has lived for the past eleven years. What does one hundred and four look like when it's time to lay the body down and die? It looks like a peaceful sleep. It looks like repose and rest, final and natural.

The singers enter the room on a song, through the parted crowd of residents in the hallway who have come to listen and to be a part of Betsy's dying journey. Our visit is an invitation for them to come and say goodbye to their friend.

Photos cover dresser tops and hang on walls. Photos of loved ones, of the 100 year old birthday party. One hundred and one. One hundred and two and three and four! Betsy's face glows with life in these photos. Now she has her eyes closed to her life and to the people around her. She has her eyes closed to her daughter who hovers in the doorway, unable to come close to her mother's bed while we sing.

"You have had your mother in your life for such a long time," I say to her as we sit together before the sing. "It must be so difficult to say goodbye." She is kind and receptive but declines my offer for her to sit beside her mother while we sing. She can't seem to form words to speak to me. Her lips quiver and her lined face contorts in a brave effort to keep tears from spilling. "Find a comfortable place," I offer. "The songs are for you too."

The songs fall from our hearts, one after another. Each one of us finds a place of comfort around the bed. I become aware of the floor beneath my feet in an attempt to feel grounded. I make an effort to slow my breathing. I take my time choosing songs to say what we can to Betsy and to the others listening. We all take our time with the songs, and settle into the silent spaces in-between breaths, in-between songs. We sing, *"I my loving vigil keeping, all through the night."* We sing, *"There are angels hovering round. I'm on my journey home."*

Betsy is disappearing beneath her covers. She appears as light as the sheets and pillows she rests upon. Wisps of pure white hair are like downy feathers on top of her head. A layer of fine hair covers her etched face like the lanugo fuzz of a newborn baby. Her skin is shriveled, her body becoming a shell emptying itself of the life force it has carried. It is time. There is no question about the rightness of this death.

Betsy's caretaker Lea moves to the bedside. She kneels on the floor and places one hand just above Betsy's chest, the other beneath the blanket to hover over her abdomen as she offers Reiki while we continue to sing. She bows her head and closes her eyes. Lea's presence beside Betsy gives the songs a sense of completion. It is alchemy. The element of change is being honored here. Mystery ripples. When Lea pulls a red rose from a vase and lays it on Betsy's chest, we sing, "*love call me home,*" and the residents hold their heads in their hands in a gesture of prayer as tears fall.

In this full moment, we choose to sing "Thuma Mina." Larry, a head taller than the rest of us, leads the call and response with his rich bass voice. The vibration of sound can be felt along the spine. We know this song well. It lives in the cells of our memory. "Thuma Mina," a chant-like song from South Africa, means heal me Lord. We don't need to say that to feel it though. *Thuma mina somandla.* The words and sounds give the singers a place to rest during our sing. It helps to keep us present, to allow us to "stay" with what is happening in a room charged with emotion. We are on familiar ground, singing a song we know well. We do not need to think about notes or words. We sing in a slow and receptive manner and offer the prayer others are whispering.

Our songs seem to carry the stories of every sing we have ever been to. Betsy's story enters this one. "Thuma Mina" now means Heal me Lord *and* there is someone who loves you kneeling at your bedside as you die, offering you Reiki, placing a red rose on your chest. There are friends all around the edges of your room praying and crying. There is your daughter at age eighty five, with a broken heart, unable to come too close because she is grief stricken. The stories of each sing enter our songs so that the next time we are around a bedside witnessing death and we choose "Thuma Mina," Betsy will be there in the room with us, perhaps helping the next one pass across the threshold, perhaps reaching out a hand to lead the way.

CHAPTER TEN

WHAT IF . . .

What if someone dies while we are singing? As in all questions about this practice, there is no way to know the best response to different situations ahead of time. We follow our heart's intuition, try to feel what is needed and respond from that place of knowing. The singing could offer just the perfect balm for the moment of death, inviting and allowing all expression of grief and release. A good leader will follow his or her instincts by watching for signs, by communicating with the family and asking good questions. If someone takes their last breath while we are around the bed, we try to remain a calm and quiet presence, we keep singing and when the time is right, slip out of the way and leave the family to say goodbye to their loved one.

Stories

❦

Right on Time

Connie and Beth were scheduled to lead a group of singers to sing for Edith. This was our third visit with her at Pine Heights, a local nursing home, where she was amidst her family in the hospice room. The leaders arrived and met four more singers. As they warmed up voices and hearts in the lobby, they learned from one of the nurses that Edith had already died. Here is Beth's report:

> It turned out that Edith had passed away in the middle of the afternoon yesterday, and there were many family and friends in the room. The administrator of the nursing home asked them if they would like us to sing and they (especially Ben, her husband) said yes, definitely. Her body was still there.
>
> Just before our group arrived at 5:15, the undertaker arrived in a hurry, ready to take the body away. I caught the guy at the elevator downstairs and asked if he could please wait for us to sing for the family, and he said "This is my seventh body today!" and headed up in the elevator with his stretcher. I spoke to the administrator, who was also passing by, and

somehow he was able to stop the undertaker moving into the Hospice room, so that when we all arrived on the 3rd floor, he was waiting at the nurses station and apologized to me!

Somehow, that particular sing, with us on the side of the room in a little "U", with Tony leading us in front, was one of the most lovely sings I have been part of! We sang "I Will Guide Thee," "Amazing Grace," "Plovi Barko," and "Angels Hovering 'Round."

The minute we started, the room of people quieted down, the family moved toward the bed, gathered around Edith, held on to each other and Edith, and quietly wept. Other people in the room also seemed to join in this connection and openly grieved with each other. There was a total release, almost like they were waiting for the music to bring them all together. Beth L said it would have been a very different experience for them if the undertaker had taken the body away before our sing. It was a pretty powerful experience. Ben was very touched by our singing.

CHAPTER ELEVEN

EMOTIONS

As we first started to visit the dying, questions and anxieties about emotional reaction followed us into the death room. What if I start to cry? What do I do when I feel emotional? How do I handle my own grief if it suddenly shows up at someone's bedside? How will I be if others start crying around me?

We are not always comfortable with the display of emotion in our culture. Just as we stand apart from death and dying, or from anything that reminds us of our fragile human nature, our emotional lives are often kept private. Most of us are uncomfortable witnessing other's outbursts of anger or displays of despair or sorrow. Grief needs expression. It wants to take some kind of shape or form in the world. Being with the dying offers us the opportunity to grow more comfortable in the presence of emotional expression. Often, grieving loved ones, who may never have shed a tear in public, will weep openly as they hold the hand of someone they love as they are dying. Being close to the dying also offers us a chance to be more in touch with the inner lives of our own hearts.

Stories

Is This Okay?

George and Carol had been married for a lifetime. During our initial conversation, Carol told me that when they first learned of George's dementia, she was determined not to lose intimacy with him. By the time we were called to George's bedside, he was days away from dying. He had been living in a nursing home for years. Carol visited him daily. She sat with him for hours, held his limp, chapped hand in her own, talked of changing seasons and migrating birds, snowstorms and mud ruts in spring on the old road. All the while they swayed gently on the glider she had brought into his room and looked out the window, side by side.

I met with Carol and George before our sing. George seemed comfortably asleep, though he stirred and opened his eyes from time to time to look into Carol's, as if to check that she was still there, keeping vigil beside him. Carol talked with me about how their lives changed as George's dementia progressed. As he remembered less and less of what his life had been, she grew more determined to hold him close. She hugged him often, held his hand, talked to him about what she knew he had once loved. But her loneliness for him was clear, as was the loss she already felt would grow enormous upon his death. I was in awe of her candor and her willingness to share her intimate experience with me as a stranger. Compassion takes my hand in moments like this, walks with me through the door and leads me to know just what to do and say.

I led the group into the room as prepared as possible. Carol had crawled into bed with George and was holding him close, the cotton sheet twisted around the contours of their pressed together forms. "Is this okay?" she asked us, and we assured her it was perfect. We also offered her our songs as prayers, knowing they were as much for her as for George, and that the music would draw them together in the closeness they already shared.

The flow of love between these two was tangible. Each one of the five of us felt surges of emotion as it moved from heart to voice. The muscles of our throats constricted. Our eyes swam. We sang anyway. George seemed calmed by the singing. Carol was tender and strong, accepting and grief-struck. She curled herself more tightly around him.

Love is powerful when it is this visible. Mary Alice could barely sing at times. She stood quietly, catching her breath, gently swaying on her feet. Peter lost some words of verses, so unlike him. Robin was a rock with her eyes closed throughout the whole sing. Tom found my eyes, pulled on me, and then looked away. I felt as if I were standing on the edge of a cliff. We took turns holding that space. We took turns being present. We hovered and we wobbled, but we all stayed. We supported each other with our voices and with our eyes. We all saw ourselves holding our own beloved in that bed where Carol held onto George with fierce love.

Waves of emotion pulled us through the verses of "Joy of Living."

*Farewell to you my love, my time is almost done. Lie in
my arms once more, until the darkness comes. You filled*

all my days, held the night at bay, dearest companion. Years pass by and they're gone with the speed of birds in flight. Our lives like the verse of a song heard in the mountains. Give me your hand, and love and join your voice with mine, and we'll sing of the hurt and the pain, and the joy of living.

Afterward, the tears came freely as we held each other in closing circle and spoke of the love we had been so privileged to witness. It didn't matter where the grief came from. What was shared in that space, as the notes fell from our mouths, was love. It did not stop us or trip us or feel unwelcome. In fact, it entered the feeling of the songs, already rich with meaning, to include the hearts of Carol and George. It personalized the sing. The emotion we all felt changed strangers into intimate friends. Compassion stood with us, kept us there, and allowed us to sing, though our hearts were broken open.

TWELVE

A Place for Grief to Rest

When Hallowell sings in a room where someone is dying, grief shows up. We have described our singing as "a place for grief to rest." But what does it mean to give grief a place to rest? Grief is not a thing with a shape and form you can hold in your hands or lay down on a bed and cover with a blanket. It changes shape. It changes color and strength. It moves in with certain smells or light, with words or melodies, and fills a room with its presence. And though it is not a physical thing we can pick up or put down, we all know that we do, somehow, carry it—in our hearts, on our shoulders, in our spirits, throughout our lives. We know the weight of grief. We also know the lightness that can follow the expression and release of it. Grief is a constant companion as we walk through our life. No one on this earth passes through life without making its acquaintance at some time.

What about our own stories, our personal emotions, the tender places in our own hearts? What do we do as a visitor, as a bedside singer, when we are standing in a bedroom where someone else's grandpa is dying? What do we do when we watch the granddaughter take his hand in hers and lift it to her lips while we are singing the words, "*no one stands alone.*" and we find ourselves back in our minds at the bedside of our own dying father. We see his hand and his eyes and hear his voice. We feel that lump that grows in the throat. We feel the ache in the heart that misses someone we love everyday. Maybe the song will stop coming out of our mouth. Maybe we will feel tears slide down a cheek. Maybe we'll miss a beat, a note, until we find a way to speak all of our own grief/love into the song so that it finds a place to rest there too.

This grief now in the room at this bedside is not ours. We are witness to it. We come here to sing in the face of it. But our own griefs are remembered and they remind us that we are not alone; we all experience this intangible thing we can't hold onto. Grief informs our love. We would not know grief without first knowing love. Doesn't the heart breaking open teach us how to love better?

We are gentle with ourselves in such moments of intensity. We might stop singing and breathe. We might need to leave the room like a cat on quiet feet. We might try to remember that we can visit our own grief later. We can change our focus, look at a stranger's face, or look at our fellow singers to find the familiar and gain strength and grounding. We can lower our eyes to the music in our hand and wait for the wave of emotion to pass so we can become present again.

Most of all, we enter the space of someone's dying knowing that we are invited guests and that we don't know who or what emotion might show up to stand beside us as we sing.

It is a gift of our practice to be reminded of our own heart's journey in life. Every sing offers this pearl to the singers. Every dying person who allows us to visit and bestow our songs provides another chance to live in gratitude for all of the love and loss we experience in our own lives. We do not judge ourselves for what we feel before, during or after a sing.

When grief comes and walks beside us, we welcome it. When its weight becomes too heavy to carry, we offer our grief a place to rest, and maybe our hearts grow a bit lighter and we remember that the source of our sorrow is the love we have known.

Stories

❧

Grief Beyond Words

In the end, it was only Gary's eyes that spoke to us. His eyes that told us how deeply he heard us, how moved he was by the music, how he wished he could sing the songs he loved with us. It was his eyes that said, I'm not afraid. Be with me. I see you. I love you.

When there is barely anything left of a physical body, the muscles weakened to helplessness, the organs no longer functioning without the aid of machines, the breath not finding its way without struggle, the spine unable to support the body in an upright position, neck falling, voice gone so even to utter a sound is no longer an option, how does one communicate the love and spirit that remain until the final letting go? Most of us can't imagine ourselves in this situation. ALS is a dreadful disease, the way it destroys a physical body, until the person residing within is almost without form. But the mind remains active and the spirit vibrant. We were shown a beautiful way to die by a man whose spirit was full of joy and gratitude for his life, even as ALS took over his body and changed the way he lived in the physical world.

Gary was a warrior. Hallowell was graciously invited to sing for him more than a dozen times over a period of two years. He was and remains a master teacher for those of us who were privileged enough to be in his presence throughout his last days here in this world. Family, friends and neighbors rallied around him, rotating schedules and care, allowing him to stay at home in the house where he lived with his beloved wife Mary and their children.

Every time we came to sing for Gary, sometimes as many as eight of us, we were welcomed by family and caretakers and received by Gary, propped in his chair like a king on his throne, awaiting our arrival. He had spent the morning preparing for our visit. He had taken a nap, so he would be rested. And he had been shaved, bathed and fed so his energy was the best possible to receive what he so loved.

Songbooks in hand, we sang one familiar song after another, taking our cues from Gary who knew our repertoire as well as we did. A musician himself with many projects, recordings and great accomplishments in his life, he honored our practice. He asked for certain songs each time we came and glowed as we sang them. He never tired of "New Jerusalem," for instance, a rousing shape note piece by Jeremiah Ingalls. Even when he had completely lost his ability to speak, Gary found ways to communicate with us. Toward the end, he would put on his special hat equipped with a laser pointer to spell out words on a board of letters his caregivers made for him. The day he pointed to "N" and we all knew immediately to turn to New Jerusalem, we were as delighted as he was, that we understood. Though he could no longer lift his mouth into a smile, we could feel the lift of it in his body.

As his disease progressed and the hat became too much to bear, Gary spoke to us through his eyes. Gary's gaze met each one of ours in turn, saying more by looking into our souls than words could ever have said. He would spend an entire song with one person. Nothing was uncomfortable about this looking because it was filled with love and gratitude. It was direct and honest. There was no way to turn away from what Gary was saying as he blessed each of us in turn.

Our singing was one small part of Gary's death. When a spirit as large and vibrant as Gary's leaves the planet, many people remaining are touched and reminded of what really matters in this world. The way friends, family and community gathered around Gary during his final years was testimony to the kindness of the human heart and spirit, a reminder of how valuable it is to work together, to create our living and our dying in ways that reflect the best of who we are.

For the last two years of his life, we visited Gary on Sunday afternoons. We sang with him and around him and for him. And we sang for his family and the many people who had shown up to learn how to care for him as his disease progressed and he needed more and more help.

His wife Mary was his primary caretaker. She was also the organizer of everything: family life, her work outside the house, and the helpers' rotating schedules. She organized household chores, meals, and the children's social lives. She held everything together, including herself. She dressed neatly in simple sweaters and slacks. Her hair was combed and pulled back just enough to frame her face.

There were no loose tendrils. Nothing seemed out of place. Until we started to sing.

At first, Mary let herself be still. She stood behind Gary with her hands on his shoulders. She sat down right beside him, pulled his limp hand into hers, looked directly into his soulful eyes, and then she crumbled. She came undone. Her shoulders rose and fell and the tears began to flow.

Our singing was a place she could let her guard down, stop organizing, worrying and holding. It was the one time in the midst of Gary's illness, facing death while his friends and family looked on, when she could feel and express the grief she carried inside of her but had so little time for. When it was time to leave, the warm hostess smile reappeared and she thanked us and walked out with us to our cars, back in gracious form, holding everything in its rightful place.

We grew to expect Mary's tears, even to welcome them. We understood that our songs were an invitation for feelings to emerge and be welcomed into the loving circle of family and friends. Emotions became a presence we could wrap in the sounds of our singing, the poetry of words sung, the way we sang through our quiet acceptance and witnessing of this family's grief. It was as if our songs helped to speak the truth of what would be a huge hole left in the heart of this family.

Mary sat across from me at dinner one night, almost a year after Gary's death. We shared pasta and tender salad greens in a quiet corner of a restaurant beside the river. I was privileged to hear the details of Gary's last night on earth. I listened to Mary's stories of her life with Gary through many years of marriage right through his dying days. And I was told that the only time she ever allowed herself to cry throughout the years of his illness was when Hallowell visited.

The songs created a resting place. Music opened a space for grief to emerge and sit quietly, among the chords. The sounds of our voices stirred the emotions and the chambers of the heart softened and opened and tears could be released.

Songs make us cry. They evoke the tears that are already there, waiting for a moment to spill, freeing the grief within us for just this little while, putting us in touch with the heart once again.

Becoming Almost Invisible

I have just come in from the market, arms loaded with bundles, about to take the dog out for a walk, when the phone rings with a request to sing. It is 3:30 in the afternoon on a weekday. We have plans to meet our kids and their spouses and the newest member of the family, two month old Nettie, for dinner and then a concert afterward. We are expected at 5:45 at the restaurant. I learn that there is an elderly woman, Catherine, actively dying in the hospice room of a local nursing home. Her granddaughter with her husband and their five month old baby are with her. She has just signed on with hospice for vigil services. We are asked to come as soon as possible.

I grab my phone and start the process of calling leaders. Ellen is sick with a migraine. Larry needs to stay home with her. Peter and Mary Alice are driving, on their way to Connecticut. I leave messages for Fred, Valerie, Mary Cay and Manny. Connie is out of town. I try every number I have for every leader. No one seems to be around on such short notice. Tom and I decide to go anyway. If we leave in the next 15 minutes, we decide, we can get there by 4:30. I am about to call on a few possible others when Val returns my call. She is at the end of her work day and says she can meet us by 4:40. She will locate her husband Mark to sing bass. We have a quartet!

On our way to the nursing home, Mary Cay and Manny call in to say they are headed north from Hadley and can meet us on their way to their evening event in Bellows Falls. I give them the room number and share what I know about Catherine and invite them to slip in and join us when they arrive.

We have come from every direction to make ourselves into a small circle of singers. Tom and I meet Val in the parking lot. We wait a few minutes in the lobby before I break off to go and meet the family and get a feel for where we are about to be. The others will meet me outside the room.

Inside the hospice room, the granddaughter Jess and her husband Rob are sitting with Catherine. Their curly dark-haired beaming baby is in her papa's arms. They have been playing our CD, dropped off that afternoon by a hospice volunteer. Catherine is unresponsive. Her body rests quietly in bed, except for the loud rattle of breath moving through dry cracked lips and a wide open mouth. Even in her stillness, it is clear that she is working hard to die. I sit beside her to tell her we are coming in to sing. I invite her to feel the songs move over her and to stay where she is while we sing, or to let go if the songs help her to do so. Jess and I talk quietly beside her and I learn that Catherine is Catholic and loves music.

By the time I leave to gather with the others, Mary Cay and Manny have arrived and we are a full group as we move into the room humming and breathing our first song around Catherine. By now, Jess and Rob are on either side of the bed and the baby is smiling and wriggling from the arms of a nurse. Her eyes open wide when we start to sing and she grows calm and watchful.

We sing "Tebe Poem." Chant-like sounds float around the room and match the rhythm of Catherine's breath. We sing, "*Blessed Quietness. Holy Quietness. What assurance in my soul. On the stormy sea, speaking peace to me, how the billows cease to roll.*" This is the song that cracks open the flood gates of grief for Rob and then Jess. Tears that had been waiting to spill for the past five days, since the beginning of Catherine's active dying stage, are now free falling. We are amazed to watch Rob fall to his knees beside Catherine, his wife's grandmother, and begin to sob. His head falls into the crook of his arm and the sounds of agonizing grief escape in loud gulps. He does not hold back. We seem to disappear, our physical presence is unnecessary in this moment. We are only the sounds of songs. And the songs have become more than words put to music. The songs have become the source from which sorrow can flow. The songs are Catherine's church congregation singing hymns. They are sunlight across moving water. They are the laughter of granddaughters and sons and babies with bright faces. They are life and loss, death and love. They sing of all that was and all that will be. They sing to this, now, this moment of beauty and death, of grief that brings a young father to his knees before an old woman he loves deeply.

Rob moves around the bed to fall into Jess's arms. We sing "Plovi Barko." We choose sounds to wrap around them, to hold them where they stand crying more quietly now, but fiercely holding on to each other. The baby, still in the arms of the nurse, is alert and glowing. We look from her shining face to Catherine's contorted and aged face to the young parents to each other. We keep singing, seamlessly. We are not unmoved, but we are still. We have become invisible. It is as if a curtain has fallen between us to offer privacy to this family as we sing.

After we sing "Sing to Me of Heaven" to say, "There will be love there, not sorrow," I lean across the bed and softly say, "are you okay?" to Jess and Rob. They understand and nod their heads to continue. My question is a way to say, we are here with you. We are comfortable with your emotions. We are compassionate. We will keep singing if you desire. We sing, "The Lord is My Shepherd," Bobby McFerrin's composition, as a prayer for Catherine. *The Lord is my Shepherd, I have all I need. He makes me lie down in green meadows, beside the still water he will lead.*

We bow as words change to hums of "Angels Hovering 'Round" and slip out of the room.

Tom and I make it to dinner on time. Our kids are unaware that we have just been somewhere we can't seem to name and have returned to share a long table with them, to pass the baby from arm to arm, and to celebrate the love that weaves our lives together. And that Catherine and her grandchildren are resting somewhere in a corner of our heart's mind.

THIRTEEN

INTEGRATION
CREATING CLOSURE, PROCESSING AFTER A SING

When we take part in a sing for someone dying, we are entering a space that is removed from reality as we know and perceive it. We enter a sort of time warp, where we stand before a great mystery. Time seems to slow way down or not to exist at all. We match our breathing to others here. We find each other's voices in harmony. We look to each other for support and connection. It is so difficult to leave this experience abruptly, without first creating a softer place to connect and transition back into our fast-paced lives.

Before we go back into the world of the living, it is essential that we create a space together for closure and for processing. There is no right way to do this. Just as each sing is different in nature and intensity, so is each closing ritual we create. It is the response to where we have been.

We may form a circle in the driveway, bow our heads, drape our arms around each other, and breathe together in a collective breath. We may circle in a hallway, lobby, parking lot, elevator or dining room. We often sing one more song together. Sometimes, if the sing was especially difficult or stirring, we might take the time to go around the circle to speak about the experience or anything it brought up for each person present. Sometimes only one person needs to talk, the rest of us becoming compassionate listeners offering support and comfort.

As we have learned to trust that we know how to be present around the bedside, we have also learned to trust that we know intuitively how to reenter the world after being so close to the edge. We create what is needed each time.

Community resources are always available to us, mostly through our area hospice. We keep an updated list of social workers, bereavement counselors and hospice staff people who are willing to offer their time and support should a sing evoke an unexpected response of grief in someone. Our hospice library is a resource for books, tapes and films. Sometimes our grounding comes in simply knowing these resources are there, backing us up and providing a cornerstone that reinforces our practice.

Stories

Outside in Circle

Once, after a particularly uneasy sing, we stood just outside of the house in the glow of the porch light. It was a cold winter night. Snow was dusting our bent heads. We huddled close together, four of us, for warmth and connection. We tried to make sense of what we had just experienced. How could we leave this sing with a feeling of calm, when what we were feeling was disturbance? In our wake, it seemed, was exhaustion. Behind the door we had just closed was a woman who struggled against her death. She seemed uncomfortable and restless in her bed. Our songs did not bring her comfort. Rather, the songs seemed to bring her out of her process, pulling her into her own memories, possibly causing sorrow more than relief. Gloria had been a music teacher and director of her own choir. Our sing for her had great potential to offer a gift.

We arrived to find a modest house in town with neighbors close by on either side. We knocked softly, anticipating a quiet entry and time for one of us to sit with Gloria for a moment before we all gathered around her to sing. A caretaker answered the door, which opened directly into the living room, and we found ourselves immediately beside Gloria's bed, set up on the first floor, just off a small contained kitchen.

Gloria was a day away from her death, though we couldn't have known. She was awake and alert and working hard to engage with us, though we offered her a time to rest while we sang. She acted as hostess from her bed, not because we were engaging her, but because it was her personality, how she had always been in her life, especially as a music teacher and director herself. Why would she be any different now at the end of her life? She wanted to direct the singers who stood before her.

Gloria could not seem to find rest in our songs. Rather she wanted to comment and engage, though the effort this took was clear to us in her exhaustion. She lifted her head after a song to share her thoughts about what she had heard. "I like that one," she struggled to say, "nice arrangement." She asked to see the musical score. She let her head fall back upon her pillow and tried to catch her breath. She closed her eyes for a brief moment. When we started the next song, intentionally choosing one she might not know, her eyes opened and her muscles tensed with the effort of trying to relate to us.

In the kitchen the caretaker moved around noisily. Nothing felt calm here and we could not help to create quiet with our songs. It was a good opportunity for us to simply accept what was happening and to be peaceful inside of ourselves with the shape of this sing, though it didn't feel peaceful. We ended our sing after just a few songs so Gloria could rest.

We sorted our coats from where they were piled on an overstuffed chair. We did our best to put them on and pull on boots without too much disruption, but everything was happening beside the bed in the space where Gloria was trying to die. Our coming and going was not gentle.

Our closing circle was essential. We hummed the song of "Plovi Barko" as the snow anointed our bowed heads. It was perfect to make the sounds without words, and to create the harmonies so softly our own sounds blanketed us. This is what we had wished for Gloria, this blanket of warmth and sound. We hummed and the snow fell. We felt the touch of gentleness as the snow powdered our shoulders. Finally we quieted enough and felt ready to climb back into our car and drive away.

We were quiet in the car, each feeling the way disappointment can enter the spirit when expectations aren't met. This was a reminder of why we practice not having expectations as well as a reminder that we have no control over what happens. If our songs fall on deaf ears or stir up unwanted emotions in someone working to die, our work is to be gentle with ourselves and to understand that our caring and efforts won't always create what we desire.

There are no "bad" sings. There is no wrong way to offer songs at the bedside. If the intention is good and the heart is present, the sing will serve in some way. Even the sings that leave us with questions or feelings of discomfort, are not damaging. There is, however, always room for growth. There can be opportunity for review and reflection and there may be ways we can improve what and how we offer our songs. We can always learn to be more present. We can grow to be quieter and to be more receptive and aware at a bedside. The bedside is a place to practice how to live well, and those who are dying before us, who have invited us here, are some of our greatest teachers.

When the Tears Come

Susan is not one to show emotion. A tall, gray haired, soft-spoken woman, she shows up for sings in a quiet state of readiness. She is always on time. She has read every email and listened carefully to the phone messages. She has never forgotten her book of music or missed a sing she agreed to be part of. She was there the afternoon we sang for Rick.

We drove for over an hour to sing on a fall afternoon, the slanting light setting off the Vermont hillsides like an impressionist painting. Rick's wife Carlene had requested the singers. Piled into two cars, we shared what we knew of Rick and his family and his struggle with ALS. The disease had progressed much more quickly than anticipated and the family was gathering from near and far to help Rick manage his final days and make decisions.

We were welcomed into a home full of wood and warmth from the stove. Rick and Carlene's son prepared food in the kitchen while ten year old Tessa sat close beside grandpa Rick, where he waited in his wheelchair, ready for our visit. A few friends had come to listen and be with Rick and Carlene. In the corner of the living room, his guitar was quiet on the stand. His hands no longer worked to strum the strings of his beloved instrument and sing the folk songs he so loved. He was a large man, ready with a smile, his dark hair soft and curly, his glasses askew on the bridge of his nose. He greeted us openly with gratitude for our time.

A natural circled formed in the long open space of the living room, with Rick at one end. Carlene joined him, pulling his hand into hers as Tessa slid her hand into his on the other side. The gathered family, including Rick, sang along on familiar songs. "I'll Fly Away" set the tone for what promised to be a lighthearted, social sing, until it changed.

How could anyone ever tell you, you were anything less than beautiful, we sang. *How deeply you're connected to my soul.* A hush fell over the room. The light changed. Rick's son found a place to sit. Our circle moved closer to Rick. Tessa, who still held onto Rick's hand, started to cry. And then so did Rick. A sob escaped his lips, fell into the room. Then another. Soon the family was crying, openly and tenderly. We kept singing. Deep breaths kept us there. We felt our feet anchored on the wooden floorboards. We caught each other's eyes and felt our voices lean against each other in the harmony we knew so well. We sang another song to stay with the grief, allow it to be where it had showed up. "Angels Hovering Round" felt right. There was comfort in the tears. There was release in the grief.

"I Still Have Joy" invited lightness back into our circle. Everyone joined in the chorus, *I still have joy oh yes I still have joy, after all the things I've been through, I still have joy.*

We felt changed leaving that family. We knew Rick did not have long to live and that his death would leave a gaping hole in the heart of his loving family. We had witnessed their love, their strength as a family, their devotion to each other. We had been invited to sing in the midst of it.

It was time for our closing circle. There was no question we all needed to be still, to try to hold each other in community, to honor where we had just been and what we were all still feeling in our hearts.

We circled in the garage off to the side of the house. We were outside of earshot of the family, enclosed in a private space. We held on. Mary Cay and I had led the sing, Mary Cay musically and I spiritually. It was up to me now to create a closing space, or at least to start the process. I asked how everyone was feeling. That was the moment Susan broke open. Her face broke first. It reshaped itself, emotions rippling like a churning sea over her usually calm features. She cried. Her chest rose and fell. She resisted and then she didn't. And we all held her.

Susan cried for all of us that day. Her tears said, there was so much grief in that room. There was so much love and emotion, such feelings of loss we almost couldn't bear to watch it. And yet we did. We sang and we witnessed. The grief belonged to this family, not to us. This was someone else's story and we felt how the heart can know compassion but not pity. Compassion seems to come directly from a place of heart, from courage. Pity is undermining. It is a feeling sorry for. It comes from believing all is not well. And yet, how can there not be wellness when the grief we feel comes from loving. Don't we all hope to live in a way that invites love like that?

We didn't need a long time in circle to complete our sing. We acknowledged each other's part and presence. We bathed ourselves in Susan's tears and expressed gratitude for everything. For emotion. For family and friends. For grief and joy. For life and death. For love. And then we drove back into the waning light to find our way home. Susan later reflected on her experience of that afternoon:

> I guess it seems obvious, but choosing to bring no expectations or assumptions when I go to a sing makes me vulnerable in a new way each time—I can

find myself suddenly reminded of my mother, or thinking of my own aging, or sometimes unexpectedly moved by the connection of a certain song with a certain person.

One evening I was in a group that sang for someone who was suffering from a progressive neurological disease, a very difficult situation. We were in a lovely warm room full of welcoming family members, surrounded by their loving presence. In many ways it was really a very upbeat occasion – our person clearly loved our being there -- and toward the end we sang a rousing "Heart of My Heart" and then our closing "How Can Anyone", and quietly left.

As we gathered in the dark outside for our circle, I just burst into tears, sobbing, while my friends held me close. I don't know why that particular setting moved me so much, or so differently from any other, but I will never forget the mixture of joy and sadness that overcame me.

I'm continually reminded that the particular situation doesn't matter – the practice of hospice singing is the same each time. Rehearsing, learning by-heart, committing to my fellow singers, being present in the room, being vulnerable, that's the point. One of our songs is the hymn "Blessed Quietness" and I've found that in the practice of hospice singing I can find what the song promises—"a peaceful habitation, a quiet resting place."

PART THREE

community

Photo: John Nopper

FOURTEEN

THE COMMUNITY AND HEALTH OF HALLOWELL

The strength and health of Hallowell as a community is essential to feed and fuel our practice. Just as it is necessary to know individually when to say yes or no to an offer to be part of a small group as a singer, to ask yourself if you are well and if you have enough inner resources to offer someone who is in a vulnerable place, Hallowell as a whole needs to remain well in order to serve our neighbors in their time of loss and sorrow. How do we keep Hallowell, as an entity, whole and healthy?

A hospice choir, like any other group serving the area that supports it, should recognize itself as a community, a whole being, within the larger community. As a group with an intention to be of service, we become like a family. We learn to care for each other, to tend each other's needs, to understand each other's weaknesses and strengths, to struggle and change. We strive to accept each other's differences and watch each other grow, individually and together. When we sing together, in rehearsal and at bedsides, the open throat, the listening heart, the harmony of notes, weave us together, with those we stand beside.

The pieces in this section address some practical issues and offer insights into what creates, maintains and nourishes Hallowell as a community and how we have learned to achieve true harmony in our practice of singing for the dying.

Stories

Source of Sound and Spirit

Tom and I live on top of a hill, two miles up a long winding dirt road in a small Vermont town. In late November, when all we see in our landscape are sticks and grey sky, when all of the leaves have fallen to the ground and the hard frost has zapped the life out of anything green or bright with color, when the hours of daylight are shorter than the hours of dark, we have to convince ourselves to go out into the world. We can forget that there is life beyond the warmth of our wood stove and the glow of lamp light in the living room. We can forget that there is more than each other in our world.

Thank God for rehearsals, for chorus and for Hallowell. Every Tuesday evening we drive down to the small church in Westminster West where Mary Cay Brass leads a community choir of 80 people. The glow from the tall windows draws us like moths as we approach. Familiar faces and exchanges with friends and neighbors as we arrive remind us that we are not alone, that we live within a greater circle of others who are part of our lives. When the singing starts, the little white church in the quiet town comes alive. It fills with sound and spirit. And it creates a connection between us that we all realize we crave.

As humans, we have a basic need for community. We want to know we belong here, in this place, in this world we travel. And we want to know we are in good company.

This village chorus, The River Singers, has been singing and performing seasonal concerts for twenty five years. It was out of this tradition that Hallowell found its original voice. Hallowell was a natural outgrowth of River Singers blending with the choir of the Guilford Community Church, directed by Peter Amidon. The larger community of these two choirs already shared so much: singers, music, friendships, spirit. When Mary Cay and Peter agreed to co-direct the Hallowell singers, a new voice emerged, with its roots already deep in the ground of the community that now supports our practice. We continue to draw from these sources of community and church choirs, in both spirit and music that finds its way into our Hallowell books.

Though the shape of Hallowell grows and changes, most of the singers who joined us at the start are still active members. Some have come and gone. Some have taken leave and returned when life allowed. Personal grief may require a member to step back for a while. But we remain a group of forty or so committed and grateful singers. Being part of the whole enriches our lives.

Wellness

It is already dark at 6:00 this November evening. We arrive early for rehearsal to turn up the heat and arrange chairs in a circle. The singers begin to arrive by ten past six. They come in chatting with each other. They take off shoes and coats, stand in small clumps around the edges of the room exchanging thoughts and stories. Someone puts the tea kettle on the stove. Conversations are making a buzz of sound. There are hugs and glad greetings as more singers arrive. We are delighted to be in each other's company, to lay our eyes on the faces we have grown to love. There is a sense, as we call each other to our waiting chairs, and to the purpose of our gathering, that we might need to schedule some social time soon.

We create intentional time for social and spiritual nourishment, a time to engage in conversation while eating bowls of homemade soup and crusty bread. We travel for a day of retreat in a new and beautiful space, during which we share a long day of singing, telling personal stories, being led in movement or ritual dance, feasting and laughing together. This is how we fill our well. This is how we grow our community in commitment and depth. The better we know each other, the more we care. The more we care, the more able we are to forgive, to tend, and most of all, to sing together in harmony.

Harmony lives beyond the sounds we make together. It shows up in the way we support each other when a sing leaves one of us shaken. It shows up in our closing circles, when we stand, physically, shoulder to shoulder, feeling the weight of what we have just witnessed together grow lighter.

One of the greatest gifts we give ourselves is the understanding that we are part of a whole. We are Hallowell. We are one voice, a breathing living entity. Each time Hallowell goes out to visit someone on their death bed, we are all there, all forty of us, standing in that small arc of four or six bodies representing the larger group. When someone tells us, "Hallowell sang for my mother," we don't remember if it was Larry and Susan, Tom and Amy who visited that bedside. And in truth, it doesn't matter. We only know Hallowell has touched that family with song and spirit. We were all there. We practice understanding oneness. We practice letting go of ego. If we were not the individual to experience that particular sing, if in our comparing minds we hear ourselves feeling unchosen or left out during the time we process sings at rehearsal, we can ask ourselves to remember that we belong. Each sing that happens includes every member of this group. In this way, we stay well. In this way, we invite our highest selves to be present each time we sing.

When we are standing around the bed of a dying woman, watching life unfold around her, do we need this person to know we are there? Do we need to be recognized? Does it matter if our name is never spoken? Or can we be as silent as the flight of an owl in the night? Perhaps we can simply show up, be witnesses, be present, bestow what we have brought and leave on quiet feet to absorb the gifts, we, in turn, have received.

Accepting and Integrating New Members

Occasionally, spaces open for new members to join the group. Hallowell does not actively seek or invite new members. When we are approached by someone who is interested in joining us, there is a consideration meeting between the leaders of Hallowell. Is this person a good match? Most often, when people are drawn to this practice, they are a good fit. We consider energy and personality. Are they gentle and willing to be led by their peers? Are they kind? Can they be in a quiet place full of charged emotion and remain present? Or do they have the potential and intention to learn these skills? Our process for accepting and integrating new members is to take our time. Often we already know a potential new member from the greater community of River Singers or Guilford Choir, in which case we have a sense of how they work with others. Other times, however, someone from outside of our circle of known people will ask to join. In this situation, we will make time for a meeting, face to face, to talk about what Hallowell does and get a feel for each other before we proceed.

We keep the wellness of Hallowell in mind. We also keep the quality of our sound in mind. From the music director's perspective, new members should be strong singers and music readers. They will have a lot of work to do to catch up with a thirteen year repertoire of songs, which can be overwhelming and daunting. Since the sound of our singing is the gift we offer, we must offer the very best sound we can. The requirement of being musically capable is as much a necessity for the incoming singer as it is for the whole group.

Once it is agreed that we will try each other out, we invite the new person to rehearsal and sing through a few simple songs with them in a small supported ensemble. During this informal audition, we hear their voice and get a sense of how they will sing in a small group situation.

Each new singer must go through a training and orientation with the leader in order to learn the ways of the practice and what will be expected of them over time. We sign an agreement that says we have covered these things:

The hospice singers offer voices and kind presence for emotional, physical, and spiritual support to individuals and families facing illness and death.

I have been informed and understand:

~ **The mission of Brattleboro Area Hospice**
~ **Appropriate boundaries with families and patients**
~ **Confidentiality requirements with hospice families**
~ **The role of the team leader for hospice singers**
~ **The need for me to monitor my own emotional processing around hospice work**
~ **Services available to me to help with my own emotional processing**
~ **How to ask questions or express concerns regarding the hospice singers**

No one is sent out to sings until they and we feel a sense of readiness. For some, it might be over a year of rehearsals and attending sings at larger events before they will be called to join smaller sings or go out to home visits. For others, the readiness comes sooner.

There is no right or wrong way to integrate new singers into a tight and strong community. For groups just starting, there may be a need for outreach into the area's choirs and musical groups. For groups already established, the concern should be the wellness of the choir as a whole. Perhaps a trial period of six months can be put into place, after which the new member is offered an opportunity to check in with leaders about whether or not the new relationship is working. Sensitivity to the new singer as well as the group is of the utmost importance. It is wise to pair up new singers with another person singing the same part of the music as they begin to make visits. Having another voice to lean against gives a singer confidence and time to breathe during moments that might take them off guard. Some new singers will be paired up for years. Just as sensitivity is called for as we sing throughout our village, it begins in the heart of our own community of Hallowell.

PART FOUR

personal reflections

Photo: Kathy Leo

FIFTEEN

REFLECTIONS—WHAT DRAWS ONE TO BE WITH THE DYING

Many paths of life have led me to my work with the dying. These reflective essays are offered as windows into what draws me, personally, to the bedsides of the dying. What teaches us in life to be present? What are the rhythms of our daily lives? How do we integrate what the world teaches us about how to live well, and how to die well? Nature has been one of my greatest teachers in life. From the wild world around me, the woods and fields I walk, the gardens I tend, the rivers and oceans I flow with, I have learned about acceptance and the natural way of life and death.

Stories

⚡

Edges

Walking along the brook in a spring rain, I am witness to winter's melt, the letting go of deep freeze, the softening, yielding, and changing of a season. In the north woods, the snow still holds onto the hillside. But alongside it, the brook is racing, roaring, tumbling over rocks, branches and mossy banks. Over the rocks it spills in gushing fury to find its way to the river. The forest floor is oozing with water, every crevice and dip has turned itself into a stream. The land is alive with awakening. It is this awakening that draws me; this mystery and reassurance of change.

Transition awakens a soul. Just when we begin to grow sleepy, complacent, seemingly accepting or well-adjusted, our world trembles and shifts and we are given a fresh lens again and again.

A large flock of robins pass over me. They dart against the gray sky through the rain. They find a place just off my kitchen to toss leaves like popping corn, searching for grubs. Spring rituals have begun. A pair of crows shout to each other from high branches. But mostly I am aware of the swell of water, the softening of the land, the mud beneath my boots, the song of the brook, and the way spring is singing itself into being.

I believe transitions are places of great learning. We are asked to wake up and pay attention. Transitions are the death of one thing into the birth of another, an ending into a beginning. Winter eases itself into spring, spring into summer, summer into fall. This is the great wheel that circles around. But within this wheel are the edges, where change is more noticeable. The edge is a landscape where the boundary between worlds grows thin and translucent. In this shimmery place we have a chance to see clearly, hear acutely, and learn more easily, if we stay alert. Great gifts are available in this wondrous place of in-between.

A friend recently gave me a close up black and white photograph of the lacy icy edge of a brook in winter. The water is flowing beneath and beside the ice. At first glance, I wasn't sure what I was looking at. What I did recognize immediately, however, was the feeling evoked in me when I looked upon this image; ice melting into water, solid into liquid, stillness into flow and light. "This is exactly how it feels," I told him, "when we stand around a bedside singing to a person dying."

Proximity to death warps and changes our concept of time. The laboring breath of a person dying creates a rhythm that everyone else in the room begins to feel and follow, so that time bends and becomes nonlinear. It's full of mystery and possibility. My friend named his photograph "Arose." Yes, I thought, this is what it feels like to be at the edge, trying to stand on moving ground.

The soft winds of spring are moving the treetops. Though the air is still chilled, the sun promises warmth and the days are full of light. The birds are so busy all around me, darting from branch to branch, tossing leaves, searching for nesting sites and materials, practicing songs. We are slipping into our next season. These are the quiet gentle beginning days of spring. We are on the brink of it, looking towards change, towards bursting gardens and spring projects; planting, raking, watching buds emerge and blossoms open while we are asleep. But here on the brink, we are merely feeling the promise of what's to come. Standing on the edge, we can rest, wait and wonder what might be before us.

When I am asked to describe what it feels like to stand in a room where someone is dying and sing our songs around their deathbed, I realize there is not enough language to give voice to this experience. We are invited into a space that feels fluid and holy, like the lacy edge of an icy brook. The sounds of our voices in harmony are beautiful, meeting somewhere in the silent spaces around the dying person's breaths. There is nothing I know to match this kind of singing. We are not performing. We have no audience. We stand in reverence and witness a soul passing. We send our notes to meet each other's in harmony, to create a soft and lovely resting place for grief, compassion and love. Nothing is expected. Nothing is assumed. We offer what we have; songs that hold stories and sound. Muscles relax, breaths come a little more easily, a struggle eases, a face softens.

Standing close to death, we notice that grief has an almost physical presence, the way it changes from sorrow to wonder to elation to despair. The force of human emotions breaks open hearts allowing love to flow outward, touching those of us who are left here, standing on the edge of this world, trying to get a glimpse into the next.

Life, Death, Walk

This is the walk when I look for death in the winter woods, when I try to reflect on the mystery of death, and how I seem to stand so close to it, but can't know what becomes of a life, of a soul. What does it feel like to witness death, to be near enough to smell it and feel its presence in a room where someone is dying? This is the walk when instead of finding death, I notice life pulsing on the brink of spring still hidden beneath the last winter storm's cover and the icy wind. Life is simmering and shimmering. Shimmering like those last beech leaves still hanging on, almost translucent now with light touching them and wind trying to catch their sails and blow them across the path.

The calendar says it is the first day of spring, but the forest says otherwise, as does the cold arctic wind blowing crisp copper beech leaves and tips of hemlock branches across the snow covered field. I am walking in my snowshoes, one determined step at a time. I can't ever get lost this way. I am wherever my next step leads me. Today it leads me into the belly of these woods I have grown to love over the past twenty five years of living on top of this hill in Vermont. At first I follow the tracks of deer, the clove-shaped imprint of their hooves sunken into the softened snow. The sun is bright in a blue sky. Everything is snapping with this spring light. Trees are talking the way they do when they are still leafless and the wind pushes them against one another. The wind is singing the song of ocean waves.

I leave the deer tracks and make my own. Before me is untouched snow. Behind me, the trail I have made with my snowshoes, a ribbon of footsteps leading from where I have already been. I am trying to be in the moment, to bring my attention to the present; my breath, the way my muscles contract and expand, the sounds of my steps in the snow, the wild wind moving through the treetops. Shadows lie across the curves of snow. They move and shift with the branches.

I have been walking for almost an hour winding my way through familiar trails. The soft snow makes the going difficult and I stop to rest. I lean my back against the trunk of a maple, sun on my face, wind blowing my hair back. I close my eyes, feel the way the tree is swaying in the wind's pull. I match my breath to the sway of the tree and feel the warm caress of sun. I seem to melt just a little into all of it until there is no separation anymore between tree trunk and my back, sun's warmth and my breath, the wind and the gentle movement of tree.

This is the way I feel when I stand at a bedside and sing to someone close to death. I am aware of who's in the bed and who's at the bedside and how the only difference between us in this moment is where we are in the room. We are all in the same world and we will all leave it when we die. Life and death are partners, I think, as I lift the branch of a baby beech tree where there are still some last leaves. The spears of buds grow longer. Soon they will push the old leaves off and uncurl new wet green leaves.

Thich Nhat Hanh, a Vietnamese Buddhist monk, gave a talk a few years ago in which he answered the question, "Is there life after death?" "Life is always with death, at the same time," he began. He sat comfortably, obviously at ease, and spoke slowly, communicating his thoughts to an alert audience. Always a natural smile rested on his face. "Life is always with death," he continued, "at the same time. Not only before. They cannot be separated. Where there is life, there is death. Where there is death, there is life. In Buddhism, it is called Inter Being. You cannot be with yourself alone. It is like the right and the left. If the right is not there, the left cannot be there. It is not possible to take the left away from the right. They want to be together. It is like above and below. Like before and after. Like you and I. They are there at the same time. Life and death happen at the same time."

I move along to the top of the rise to visit the old oak tree. This grandfather helped me navigate my way through this woodland when I first came here. I would find my way back by looking for the tall, reaching branches at the top of the hill. I once saw a raccoon curled in the crook of its branches, a breathing ball of fur napping in the arms of the oak. Now the great oak has fallen. This past fall, a windstorm snapped the hollowed out trunk and the tree fell, downhill from where it stood for years. There is a clearing now where its branches once filled the sky. I climb up onto the back of the horizontal trunk. There is something magnificent about the death of this tree that has lived more decades than I have, something majestic and wonderful and achingly sad. Grief lives where the oak once stood, where I have come for years to write, to meditate, to cry or laugh, think or rest. And I feel love here; love for this place that has offered me refuge, and for this old oak. Maybe grief and love are partners too. Maybe they need each other to lean on, in order to exist. Like right and left. Like above and below. Like you and me. Like life and death.

As I near my house, flocks of birds greet me with song and flutter; doves, nuthatches and chickadees. The finches feathers are turning yellow. How do they know this is the first day of spring despite the cold air and deep snow? Light touches everything. Smoke flows from the chimney. The wind chimes answer the wind. The sun promises warmth soon. The finches know. The world is pulsing with life, with death and life again.

What We Bring Home

We are at a house concert, sitting on the top floor of a barn framed in wooden beams, windows open to the outside breeze. Chairs are lined up and we sit comfortably, tenderly listening to Linda Worster from Nantucket sing about Spirit Friend. We are at Edie's house, where she lives alone now that her husband died, just over a year ago. This concert is in Ted's memory. The late August gardens are golden and violet with prairie cone flowers tall on strong stems alongside purple asters. Squash vines roll onto the lawn. Tomatoes are red on the vine. There is beauty here in this lovely home.

Edie's face wears a blend of both the joy and grief she feels as her friend Linda sings the song she requests. Her eyes are bright with knowing and emotion. The song brings to mind and heart all of those I miss, she tells me later. Her beloved cousin comes and her late husband Ted. We all listen with the ears of our hearts, and make space for the memories of those we have loved and who have died to come and sit in the spaces between us. As Linda sings "Spirit Friend" our hearts seem to grow, collectively, larger.

Once again your spirit comes,
sits down by my side.
Once again his spirit comes,
and joins your love to mine.
And I hear the song you're singing,
even though I am alone.
Have I told you that your gentle soul,
brings such comfort to my own.

Sometimes I get lonely,
my heart forgets your sound.
I search that heart for peace.
The peace is nowhere to be found.
And if I listen with an inner ear,
I can hear your song again.
Have I told your gentle soul,
just how strong your love has been.

I can almost see you smiling.
I can almost touch your hand.
There's no need for words to say,
what only spirits understand.

Cause when I need someone to talk to,
I can sense you drawing near.
Your loving lingers at my door,
though you're miles away from here.

I can swear I hear your music
and our voices as they blend.
I hope you know, dear gentle soul,
how much it means to be your friend.

The room is so still with listening you almost hear the tears sliding down cheeks, being wiped away with the backs of hands. Beside me, Tom reaches for my hand. He looks over at me and we fall, for a grateful moment, again, into each other's closeness. We are acutely aware of the fact that we are both here, physically, in this world, sharing the afternoon, this music, our lives. And we are aware of Edie, sitting alone, missing her husband, calling him to draw near.

This is the kind of awareness that follows me home from every sing I attend. It greets me in the morning as my eyes and ears open to the day. Tom is still here. I woke up. He woke up. And there it is, beside us, the knowing that this won't always be true. That there will come a day when one of us leaves. Is it called sorrow? Is it called joy? Is it an anticipation of grief? Whatever It is, it deepens what we know, what we do, and how we live.

Some days the weight of emotion after a sing can follow us home. Most times, this emotion transforms into gratitude and we leave a sing feeling joyful, almost ecstatic. But there is a lingering awareness that has grown in all of us over years of standing close to death and grief. It has no name or shape. But it is there, a constant presence in our daily lives.

I am aware that Tom is here today. He is working in the bee hives in his white suit. Smoke from burning wood shavings and pine needles fills the late summer air and settles the bees. Honey drips from the frames.

In the kitchen, steam infuses the sunlight streaming through the south windows as the smell of ripe tomatoes and fresh basil seeps into the wood beams. Clean quart jars gleam on the counter, lined up for the canner. Baskets overflow with red and green peppers, cucumbers, zucchini, plums. Sunflowers in a blue glass jar lean against the window. I am dancing with the tomatoes, chopping and swaying my hips to the music playing.

I lay down my knife, leave the chaos of fall kitchen, and hop on my bike to ride through the mowed paths that lead to where Tom is, in the heart of the bees. The need to lay my eyes on him is simple. It is a love for our life, our shared days in the sun. A way to keep breathing. He is dancing with the bees.

The bedside where death is close, is a charged place. It offers us, as onlookers and visitors for now, prayer, song, reflection, grace. It also drains us at times. It makes us weary and worried. It brings us to our knees with the clear and perpetual understanding that death will come. It will come to those we love. And it will come to each of us.

Do we grow more comfortable with this truth as we spend years in the practice of visiting bedsides of the dying? Perhaps. Some days. And yet, as in all practices, there are moments when we stumble, forget the words, the moves, the way. We lose our confidence or our faith in the way things are. Sorrow can be so large in the space of grief that we all grow short of breath.

Our practice is to keep showing up. And we do, with songs on our lips, with our hearts curious and alert. We take home with us the gift of knowing that our daily lives are sacred and our ordinary days are extraordinary.

PART FIVE

other voices

Photo: John Nopper

SIXTEEN

SINGERS' VOICES

I am in eighth grade chorus. We are sitting in sections, bass, tenor, alto and soprano, on the stage in the empty auditorium. Mr. Imperial, fresh out of college, is the music teacher. He is tall and thin and wears sneakers and khaki pants. We have just sung the Beatles' song, "Here, There and Everywhere." The sopranos, as usual, have the melody. A familiar and favorite song of mine, I sing out. I really sing out. I let my voice open and soar and sing the notes I already know. I feel ecstatic singing out loud. I am loving the sound of my own voice. Mr. Imperial is not. He stops the choir. He points to Cindy beside me, and then to me. He pulls us out to stand in front of the chorus. The boys are snickering. Heat rises up my entire body, colors my chest, my neck, and my face, the color of beets. "These voices," says Mr. Imperial, "do not blend."

He is right of course, though there is no need for shame. Cindy's voice is rich and clear and makes me think of cascading water over rocks or wild birds in early spring. I don't mind not-blending beside her. What could become a traumatic moment is saved by Cindy's confidence. She tosses her head back and laughs. Mr. Imperial grins and sends us back to our seats. He isn't exactly being mean, just young and pompous.

I learned something that day, about leadership and kindness, but more importantly about blending in a way that makes the whole better. I didn't stop singing. But I started listening more carefully to the other voices around me.

In Hallowell, we practice listening to the other parts. During rehearsal, we mix ourselves up and travel around the room while singing "Deo Gratias", sopranos and altos among basses and tenors. We try not to hear our own voice, but to become one voice. And yet without individual voices, we would not create the rich sounds of a choir. It takes all of us to make harmony.

Something was missing while writing this book. It was the absence of other voices. As the stories came, I felt myself singing a solo on these pages. I was not blending. I missed the others' notes that make the chord.

In this section, you will hear the sounds of the singers' voices, individually and in concert. Hallowell is a choir, after all. Hear the voices of some of the singers through their own words as they reflect on questions and share personal experiences.

WORDS FROM OUR MUSICAL DIRECTORS:

Peter Amidon

Forming Hallowell with Kathy Leo and Mary Cay Brass has been a completely unexpected shower of blessings from the start. I, who have feared death because life is so wonderful, have the privilege over and over of singing for individuals and their families who seem to be at peace that their life is ending. Each visit brings me closer to accepting my own death. The actual hospice sings are as healing for me as anything else that I experience. Being in the room with the singers and family can be timeless. Afterwards I feel calm, centered, joyful, fully alive. I love our group of singers, and I love how the songs we have sung for two or five or ten years go deeper and deeper inside us.

Mary Cay Brass

Being a member and co-musical director with Hallowell has significantly changed my relationship with death. Most of my life I have been quite protected from death. I come from a long lived, healthy family and had never been forced to really look at it. When the invitation came to be a musical director of Hallowell, I jumped at it as a way to meet death head on, over and over again and to watch and observe and grow from what came up inside me in response to countless opportunities to be with the dying, their families and loved ones.

Being with death and dying is a practice that can and really should be part of our everyday lives. In many cultures people live much more closely tied to all the seasons of life; living with animals, caring for our elders in our homes. Our culture has a way of sanitizing the end of life, looking at it as a failure instead of the natural transition that it is. We have so many opportunities to practice with "little deaths" in our lives: endings of relationships, jobs, friendships, disappointments. All opportunities to grieve, let go, move on.

All of this practice was particularly helpful to me in attending to my own mother's passing. It was a very quick process of 17 days from diagnosis to death. We had very little time to get used to the idea that she was dying. It was all moving so fast. What was really amazing to my siblings and myself was how at peace, at ease, she was with the fact of her own death. She was simply ready and had been for some time so her last days were quite peaceful, even joyful, as she welcomed everyone in for good byes. Some of us from Hallowell had the unique opportunity to do a sing for her and my father and siblings via Skype. Even through computers the power of song for them and for us was quite powerful and moving.

It is a joy and honor to be a Hallowell leader with both Kathy and Peter. We have such an easy flow among us and our combined skills enrich, support and sustain the group. It is also a privilege and honor for all of us to be invited into the most intimate and sacred of spaces – the home or room of a dying person. I am in awe every single time. In awe that families invite us, in awe at the power of song to move energy in myriad ways in that space, in awe of all of our commitment to making this happen over and over again.

WORDS FROM SINGERS:

Fred Breunig, tenor, has been a member of Hallowell from the beginning in 2003.

I came to Hallowell from a unique place—in caring for Dinah during her final years, I had what one friend characterized as "a graduate course in dying." So I was already comfortable being at a deathbed and I had lost my fear of death. I also had a number of experiences with spirit.

After Dinah died, many people thanked me for sharing our lives during that time, "Well, I'm glad you feel that there is a gift for you there. But I was really just doing what I needed to do for myself."

Hallowell provides an opportunity for me to serve, to help me manifest my spiritual essence at the personal level, to be fulfilled. I feel so grateful to Hallowell. It has given me the chance to be connected with spirit, with love, with end of life, with the birth of my spiritual awakening, and with Dinah.

I remember the moment that I realized that I was no longer afraid of Dinah dying. During August of 2002 the doctors thought that Dinah might have only a few weeks left (she actually responded to a new treatment and rallied for another several months). One day, in the middle of a moment of grieving for her, a thought occurred to me. I had been so close with Dinah for thirty years, I wonder if I might be able to learn something more about what happens to people after they die. Might I be able to get a glimpse of heaven, of the spiritual realm, of life beyond the veil? Might I be able to communicate with Dinah? That hope of new possibilities became a silver lining to the reality that I would soon be losing her.

Contemplating that, I found that I no longer feared the inevitable, her death; I accepted that it was going to happen and began to wonder, full of awe, what might be in store for her afterwards. It was only a moment more before I realized that the same would be in store for me some day and then, in another moment, that I did not fear my own death.

Being comfortable around the dying and not fearing death itself have enabled me to be very present at bedsides. At a sing, I like to focus my attention on the person for whom we are singing, visualize her journey, think about what he might be about to experience. Three days before she died, I was able to glimpse through Dinah's eyes the banquet that was laid out for her, the pansy-colored lights, the throng that awaited her. Is that what will welcome this person? Or some other equally magnificent setting?

Joan Shimer, soprano, is the elder of Hallowell. She joined us in 2009. She offers two stories of sings that she found particularly moving. Nearing the End:

February 9, 2012

She lies in her bed alone; her husband sits across the room in a chair. We have come to sing for them for she is dying. She coughs lightly, and says, "I think I might be dying." And then, "Am I going to die coughing?" We sing some peaceful songs. Her husband stays in his chair. She fidgets a bit, coughs a little, and says it again, "Am I going to die? I think I am going to die." Our singing time is short. Kathy speaks gently with her and says goodbye and thank you. We leave and put our arms around each other in the parking lot outside. One of us says, "She seems pretty feisty to me." Two days later we learn that she has died. No one held her hand or comforted her as she lay there. We are glad we had brought music.

February 9, 2012

He is thin and wasted but greets us at the door wearing his broad smile and his hat. We know that his prognosis is for a short life. He wants to live to see his daughter graduate from high school this June. He has chemotherapy weekly. We come in and arrange ourselves in a semi circle opposite the couch in the small living room crowded with a pile of tires, a large TV, a walker, and several lovely paintings on the wall. As we organize, his daughter and her mother emerge from the kitchen, cross the room and go out, leaving us to our music. L settles himself on the couch, puts his feet up on a foot rest, leans his head back on the couch, closes his eyes and smiles while we sing - for nearly half an hour – some lively, some peaceful. L just sits there smiling. When we feel it is enough, we gather to leave. L thanks us and says goodbye. We have been singing for him monthly, for at least three months now.

Manny Mansbach, tenor, joined Hallowell in 2012

Mary Cay had been with Hallowell from the start, and as musical co-director had been to countless bedside sings. I was a pretty new member of Hallowell, and Mary Cay and I had been partners for only nine or ten months on the day she received "The Call". Her mother Camille had advanced pancreatic cancer, and it was clear the end was near. A few days later Mary Cay flew to be with the family in Minnesota, and I joined her there, never having met her folks. When I walked into the family home, her mom—in pajamas and robe and clearly weakened—beamed at me, and with a twinkle in her eye and delight in her voice said, "Well, helloooo… and goodbye." Such a powerful statement of equanimity and acceptance of what was to come. I replied, "Well, how 'bout we just start with hello?" It was a wonderful exchange despite the circumstances.

Fast forward less than a couple of weeks later: about seven or eight singers including the recently returned Mary Cay gathered at our home to embark on a new variation in our hospice singing—the Skype sing. We gathered around the laptop perched on the kitchen table, viewing Mary Cay's father looking bewildered and wracked with grief and anxiety, sitting in a chair with his hand reaching out to touch his mostly unconscious wife of 62 years lying in the bed next to him. Two of Mary Cay's siblings were present in the background, supporting their father, moving in and out of the room, taking in as much as they could. We sang "Over the Rainbow".

Tears flowed both in Minnesota and Vermont. I was grateful for the other singers' voices during those moments when I became choked up and had to pause. Even for the more seasoned singers, sharing this music for one of our director's parents was new, intimately poignant. When Peter led "On Eagle's Wings", a longtime favorite of Camille's, both rooms were crackling with emotion. The intensity was such that we stopped after only three songs—simply because that was enough. The connection had been made, the ministry ministered. It may have been one of the most emotionally challenging sings for some of us, but I don't think anyone there would dispute that it was also exquisite, just as right as could be. Our last song felt truly fitting: "Angels Hovering Round."

Amy Harlow, soprano, has been a Hallowell member since its beginning in 2003

My experience with Hallowell has been multi-tiered. I remember Kathy proposing her idea of the choir soon after Dinah's death and I knew right away that there would be reasons why singing for Hospice would be a positive experience for me. At the time I had no idea what those reasons would be, but I loved the whole idea of it.

Soon after we began rehearsing and going out into hospitals and homes of our hospice patients, I received a call from my step-mother explaining that my father had suffered an aortic aneurism and there was nothing they could do to save him. I was in Vermont and my father was in California. I left immediately and within ten hours I arrived at the hospital in San Francisco in time to say good-bye, and to know that he knew I was there. His dying was swift, and clinical, and cold. There was little empathy from the hospital staff and although a social worker came to explain what was happening, there was no comfort in our experience. My step-mother and step-sister and I had to make decisions about morphine and comfort levels with no understanding of what were doing.

My father passed after being suddenly moved from the intensive care unit to a room in a remote area of the hospital. I will never forget, and will always be haunted by the look in his eyes as he was wheeled swiftly over the gap into the elevator on his way through the hospital. We were alone, the four of us in that room as he took his last breaths and we sat there unsure of what to do. We had to get the nurse to come to the room. My step-sister and I said goodbye to him and we left the room so that my step-mother could have some time alone with him.

After we spent some time in a chapel alone, processing the experience and trying to make sense of it all. Then my step-sister and I walked out of the hospital in one direction while my step-mother took a cab home and I remember thinking as I walked down the street, "My father's body is in that building, and I am walking on this street where life goes on, where nobody knows what we have been through, while I am deeply grieving." Within another eight hours, I was on a plane headed back on the redeye flight to New England.

It so happened that there was a wedding the next day. It was the wedding of my dear friends, Larry and Ellen Crockett. They were to be married during the church service at the Guilford Church and we, their musical friends, were going to sing for and with them. I arrived in Boston and drove directly to the church. The glory of the voices and the community and the event contrasted so deeply with the experience that I had just been through that the lack of sleep was irrelevant. I was embraced and held by Hallowell friends who had no idea of the details of my experience, but who knew the energy and love that is necessary for someone who has lost a parent.

This is the reason, I thought, this is the reason why I was called to sing with Hallowell. It was about knowing that there is somebody there for you in some sweet and wonderful way when you think that your pain and loss is unbearable. It's the family of singers who appear for you, like angels, and carry you for a while so that you can experience grief, but also so that you don't disappear. You are acknowledged and held and supported and sung to, like a child in the arms of her parent.

Annie Guion, soprano, joined Hallowell in 2006

Singing with a purpose changes the act from a performance to a gift, a service. And it requires community, all of the singers working together with guidance from trusted leaders, to deliver that gift in just the right way for that person and that moment. I love the moment on the way to a sing when I let go of all the days accumulated tasks and to-do lists, and just focus on breathing and the joy of being alive. It is a great re-calibration back to center, back to living in the present and remembering to be grateful for each moment of life.

Gill Truslow, soprano, joined Hallowell in 2013

The experience of singing in rehearsal with this devoted group of caring people moves me deeply, and deepens my commitment to this practice as stories are shared about the healing power of our singing to families and the peace it brings to those leaving this life with beauty and grace. I am so grateful to be part of this community and hope to be able to offer more service in the future.

Beth Spicer, soprano, joined Hallowell in 2011

One thing I was thinking this morning as I lay in bed, wide awake at 4:15am with Things To Do racing around in my head: I began thinking, what it is that Hallowell means to me? One thing that I love is the joining of souls in a meditative way, through song, with someone who is at end of life and right there, in the moment; our focus is totally, completely on lifting them with song. We all have to quiet our thoughts and bodies and come together in quiet song. For me, we are there for each other and for ourselves. It's a healing experience for all of us! Hallowell is a gift.

Leslie Goldman, alto, joined Hallowell in 2012

I always look forward to Hallowell rehearsals. The members of the group are so full of kindness, generosity of spirit and love that it is an honor to be with them. I leave with a sense of peacefulness and connection every time.

I have been able to sing at bedsides, funerals and nursing homes in the last three years and every time I feel I have made a small contribution to the great cycle of life. The bedside sings are the most profound and for a brief time there is a connection between the client, their family and the people I am singing with.

One of the hardest things is to get into a car after a challenging sing, and get on with life. On occasion when I get home, I have to take a moment for some tears at the inevitability of the end-of-life, an emotional example that had just been before me.

Larry Crockett, bass, has been an active member of Hallowell since 2003

I am aware of the visual dimension - what is the physical affect of the person for whom we are singing, what is happening with family members, with the other singers, what is in the room, what is on the walls, etc. I just try to be tuned in to all of that. I also try to be very tuned in to our sound as a group. I am also sometimes aware of an unseen and unheard dimension, unseen presences, "angels hovering 'round."

I have been in sings that have moved me emotionally, perhaps because they were persons whom I knew, or because some aspect of the setting reminded me of the night my late wife Shirley died. I have felt tears coming, but I don't remember getting to the place where I felt I needed to leave the sing. I guess I just sang through my emotions. I think I probably shared something of what I was feeling in the closing circle and, of course, one always finds support in those circles!

I feel more at peace with death. Death feels more like a friend. This raises some tension with my faith tradition, because in at least some strains of Christian theology - especially the Apostle Paul - death is the enemy. I can see the reason for that, but I personally no longer feel that way about death. I think - I hope - that I will welcome death when it comes to me. Being present at so many bedsides where someone is on the threshold of life has made death seem so much more like a part of life, a natural experience. Of course, I know that death can be violent and unwanted and unexpected, but the experience of singing at the bedside has taken the "sting" out of death, in a way.

Calvin Farwell, bass, joined Hallowell in 2010

I have been at several emotionally challenging sings. These have been when the subject was somehow easily identified with me: a friend of mine, a look-alike for a member of my family, a teacher, a scientist, a singer, a squash player, a hockey player, etc. Perhaps some part of me is imagining that I'm the one who is dying. In these cases, my singing mechanism starts to misbehave, I can't breathe properly, I feel like crying, and I have to take a measure or two "off". These "fits" don't last very long. However, whenever one has occurred, I have brought it up in our after-sing circle, and have found that my fellow singers were a sensitive and seasoned support group.

Before joining Hallowell, I had hardly any significant relationship with death. Of course, given my age, I had experienced the event of death on numerous occasions, as my four grandparents, my mother, and numerous aunts, uncles and some good friends had all passed away. I had experienced the event of death as a sudden loss. But these events all happened at a distance. I was present neither at the death itself, nor during the weeks and months approaching the death. I was only present at memorial services and burials. But I had no relationship with death as a process—the transformative process of dying, of letting go of life.

At the age of 69, I retired from my teaching career. One of my reasons for retiring was so that I could spend more time with my father, who was then 98 years old. About this time, I joined Hallowell, and began to sing for people in various stages of the process of dying. This experience was invaluable. I was visiting my father often, and couldn't help but notice how, little by little, he too was loosening his grasp on his earthly existence. This was both painful and beautiful to watch. But when he finally (and uneventfully) died at the age of 100, I knew that, for over two years, he had been preparing for this event, and that he was ready. I, too, was ready.

Valerie Kosednar, soprano, Hallowell member since 2003

When I am called to be the music director at a sing I strive to stay fully present with the mood and feeling in the room, as it may shift and change throughout the sing. Fully open and present, I am able to make sensitive and intuitive song choices in accordance with the ebb and flow of this energy in the room. I also hold the responsibility of providing the singers what they need to be their musical best. The musical direction, however subtle, needs to be clearly communicated in order for the singers to offer their best singing, which is ultimately our greatest goal and our greatest gift.

Susan Barduhn, alto, started singing with Hallowell in 2010

Singing with Hallowell has made me more thoughtful. When we are singing – at a bedside or during rehearsals – I am experiencing the music and the words and the presence on different levels, all of which can exist simultaneously, as providing new shades and hues for the whole.

Far from being at all difficult, this is one of the joys. There is so much presence going on to enter into and be part of in creation. It is a poignant, honorable space, created by individuals devoted to one purpose: being present.

Terry Sylvester has been singing alto with Hallowell from the beginning in 2003. She responded to my questions from Moldova where she is working for The Peace Corps for two years.

Being part of Hallowell grounds me, even here.

The night before I left for Moldova, luckily I put both of our records on my gizmo so I can listen to this music here, but most especially, sing along! And when I do I realize how much my BODY and SOUL is missing singing with other people! How this feeds me in such a physical way, and with Hallowell it crosses over into other ways as well.

And I know that almost all of it is informed by my experience of being with my dying mother years ago now, and being so glad that the music takes me to that sad wonderful place. It was a glorious early fall morning and the window behind her bed opened to a sparkly garden of orange and green and purple, so shimmery.... our CD had been playing for a few days and it felt like the music was another familiar person in the room.

Now when I hear this music from so far away it connects me to her and to all of Hallowell and then goes beyond that known company to reach out to the people here. The words remind me to see in them "How could anyone ever tell you that you are anything less than beautiful..." when I see their missing brown teeth and filthy hands and feet from working in the fields all day or from having no water at home to wash with...but it also comforts me on a Thursday night when I picture singing with everyone in a great big circle and feeling like I'm there and going to the best of church services ever.

A few weeks ago we had a Mid Service Training, and there was an exercise to write down a secret, maybe a feeling you have had since being here and shared with no one, about anything, and the first thing that came to my mind was that I wasn't afraid to die. I have no idea where that came from, but I know that my Hallowell experience has informed me in a very real way that I have nothing to be afraid of.

Connie Woodberry, alto, has been a member of Hallowell from the beginning in 2003

We sang for a woman at Vernon Green. There were family pictures and embroideries hung around her bed. There was a plaque with neat handwriting on the wall next to her bed. "Norma loved to grow and can vegetables. She loved music and sang in her church choir. She had many dear friends. Most of all Norma loved being a mother." As I looked at the woman lying in the bed, eyes closed, unresponsive, wispy white hair around her wrinkled face, I knew I was her. There I was lying in bed, dying. And it was okay. She had lived a full life. She loved her life and the simple daily chores that made up her life. And whatever fear I have ever had of death fell away.

Ryan Murphy, hospice care coordinator for Brattleboro Area Hospice.

Hallowell creates a sacred space and then fills that space with love and reverence. I have often had the privilege to be present when a Hallowell group will very gently and sensitively engage people they are meeting for the first time and then move into delivering their gifts of solace and peace.

In these moments people facing death and often the people whom they love and who love them experience a transcendence of their immediate circumstance. In these moments I believe their eternal essence may emerge and is recognized and honored. This is often a powerful visceral experience of release and of an outpouring of love that moves people in ways they could not have imagined and creates very precious shared memories they hold in their hearts.

The spontaneity and sheer beauty of these moments of such very human connections are, for me, the Heart of Hallowell. I am so appreciative of and grateful for their ministry.

Call and Response

This morning I heard the call of chickadee, the early spring call after deep winter freeze begins to imagine it will let go and the light returns by degrees each day. I went out in the dim early light, before color emerges, and stood still in the crisp cold with an armful of wood because the chickadees were calling across the morning. I paused to listen. Their lilting two note song, back and forth, one calling out, the other responding, stirred me. The seasons keep moving. The days grow dark and then light again. The wood pile diminishes. The chickadees sing to the changing world.

I needed to ask permission to use the stories I wanted to share. How do I approach this, I wondered. How can I ask Beverly to read an emotional piece of writing that speaks of her son Mark's dying? A wash of emotions passed through me as I pushed "send" the first time. There was no writing attached yet, only a note wondering how she would feel reading of our time with him during his dying. I sent a letter giving options to say no or to change anything that felt awkward or disturbing, or to change names and details to offer anonymity.

My intention for these stories is to offer insight into the quality of our practice, but most of all, to remember each person we were honored to be with during their dying. The stories remind us that each sing makes us larger somehow, invites us to open and feel brightly alive in our senses. I hope these stories touch and teach. The families, those who made the invitation for us to share the most intimate experience of love and loss, must give me their blessing.

Bev agreed to read the piece "The World Grows Quiet." The second time I pushed "send" with the story attached, I felt as if I had opened a gate into the unknown. My world felt quiet. I had sent my words into the silence, not knowing how or even if they would be received by the most important recipient of this particular story. The chickadee sends her song into the open sky and waits for a response. I waited. I trusted. And the response came back, bringing with it a new friend's heartfelt honesty and emotion. The connection, already felt through our time with Mark, deepened.

How can any of us know the difference our intentions and actions make to others? Our lives move mysteriously beyond us.

I wrote:

> Dear Bev, I wish you had been there when we visited and sang for Mark. If you have questions or concerns or if any of this raises anxiety or just doesn't feel right, I am glad to leave it out of the book or to make any changes you and any others in your family suggest. If, after you read it, you decide I shouldn't change his name, I won't. I want to honor Mark's story, your loss

and grief, and the love he shared through his life and his death. Although I haven't met you, your son was a friend and a teacher in so many ways. And whether or not we use his story in the Hallowell book, I want you to know that our time with him moved each of us deeply. He was so full of grace. with gratitude, Kathy

She responded:

Oh Kathleen I am sitting here in the tiny living room of our very small house at the lake. A place Mark dearly loved and the only place where I am truly at home and the real me resides. I guess the only other place this old country girl is comfortable is at the Quaker school where Mark went and where I teach. Anyway I tell you this to give you some context for where I read your exquisite writing. I am surprised I can see and type through the tears. What a gift this writing is to me. You have allowed me into more of Mark's world as it slipped away. I cannot thank you enough and I long to meet you. Steve, Mark's dad, has not read this yet

In Marks own words, I am the spiritual one, the one who truly believes that Mark is on his heavenly journey with my father whom he sort of idolized. Mark was only 8 when daddy died. I am rambling. But I somehow know that that is ok with you.

I will ask Steve for his permission for you to use this as you wrote it and to use Mark's name. You already had my permission even before I had the courage to read this. I will call you when we get back to what I call the "outside of Philadelphia" house. I would love to talk to you. You have let me into times when I was not there with Mark and for that I thank and love you. Ok. More tears so I will stop writing for now.

I am off to sleep in my bed against the window from which I can see the stars. If it were warmer, I would sleep outside which I love to do. So for now good night. I will show your writing to Steve to get his permission but my guess is that it is fine. Your poetry at the end was/ is exquisite!

A hug for you. Bev

About a week later:

Hi dear Kathleen.

Steve just read your beautiful and of course wrenching words. We cried of course. We don't cry together much. We each have our own way I guess. Steve is a man of few words but "powerful" is the one he used. You are free to use this with Mark's real name.

Your writing is a gift to us and a beautiful heartfelt tribute to Mark. Please publish it with our blessings. I would love to read your finished book if I may and I look forward to the cd. May God bless you and yours for a joyful holiday season. The world is a better place because of people like you.

Bev Green.

At first, I could only send out one piece at a time. Each one flew off like a prayer, full of hope, not knowing if it would be answered. It was almost too much for me to wait. This was not about feeling impatient. I was learning how to trust in a way that was bigger than I could have imagined. I was asking people to be vulnerable, to revisit a time of grief that changed their lives. And of course, I wrote the stories from my perspective. Our personal experience is not always shared with others who may have stood right beside us at the bedside.

What I know in my wisest moments, is that the kind of grief we witness through most of our sings is grief laced with love. The families that make a space and invitation for singers who are strangers to surround the bed of a dying loved one and be amidst them at such an emotionally rife time are generally open to sharing their story with the world. When we share the stories of our hearts, we give others permission to do the same. We make changes that brighten the world and connect us to each other through our most humble and human qualities.

As the responses started to come back, one after another, I realized trust. I sent out two at a time. Genie answered immediately with these words in response to Equanimity:

> Well, you were right. My heart did soar reading your words AND I cried. I was again reminded of those extraordinary visits from your group; the feeling of acceptance, warmth, love coming from all of you as you sang. And the songs couldn't have been more perfect; how did you know to choose the exact songs that Jeff and I would identify with so completely. It

reminded me too, of how in just two short visits to the farm, you seemed to absorb our situation and understand and feel so fully what was in our hearts! I have felt since I first saw you that the truly amazing thing about the Hallowell singers is their open hearts and minds that come into lives at the most profound and intimate moment near death to witness and bring joy through music. What a gift, Kathy. Or, speaking for myself and for Jeff, what a gift to our family friends and the two of us. And now I have this wonderful piece of writing that beautifully reminds me of the last week. I hope it will speak to others when they or their family member faces death. It can be a joyful time, a life filled time in the midst of the sadness. Jeff really showed the way to those around him! I watched those other people dying in the hospital, grasping and gasping for every minute, demanding the most sophisticated medical help. And then I think of Jeff in his living room, looking out at the cows, writing his memoir early each morning, spending his days talking with, and being with, his dearest friends and family. And with your group surrounding him, then singing to him from the balcony. Again, such a gift! Thank you again, Kathy, as you have brought to life those final days!

My trust grew and I sent out three or four at a time. "Children at the Bedside" required permission from five living children. Four sisters and one brother agreed they wanted the piece included and they wanted both Harry and Luella to be called by their names. Kate wrote:

> Thank you so much for sharing this beautiful piece. I wanted to read it when I had some uninterrupted time and space, so I waited until today. It does bring up lots of emotions, but thankfully my parents both had beautiful passings, and the Hallowell singers were such a part of that experience. We felt so lucky to have all of you with us. It sounds like the book will be a wonderful way to reach out to people about end of life issues, and has the potential to help so many. My mother would love that you are writing down the stories.

All of the siblings agreed to share the story. Nancy replied to me personally as well:

> Dear Kathy,
>
> My sister Kate forwarded the beautiful piece you wrote about our mom. I think you captured the setting & emotion of the time we spent saying farewell to our dear Luella (and Harry). I love the way you wrote about her style & grace. She was a lovely woman and I miss her very much- she is in my thoughts daily.
>
> I also cherish remembering those moments in the hospice suite with both of my parents. I can't say enough about the physical setting & how it accom-modates & supports a grieving family. It really makes

it possible for the family to become part of the death experience, which I feel is so important.

The role that the Hallowell singers played for us as a family is also a very valuable one. Your presence was an enormous GIFT in many ways. Your presence as a group was strong & comforting. The compassion & love that each of you are filled with, transcended & moved through your beautiful voices and touched us as we sat in the sacred space. By being physically present with us, you gave us such a powerful, yet reassuring message.

I don't know if you are aware of what your singing does for the grieving family?

As I'm writing this, I'm wondering if you may even want to include a chapter from families who have experienced the Hallowell singers as part of the death & dying process... Just a thought.

One more thing. I was with each of my parents when they passed. I am an RN and have spent a lot of time with folks who are ill, as well as with those who are dying. I am very comfortable with it. Not to say it isn't difficult, but it is an honor.

I knew my mom was going to pass the night she actually did. We had been taking turns staying over & it was one of my sibling's turns to stay. But, my sibling declined & said she would stay the next night. I told her how I didn't think there would be another opportunity.... I was happy to stay & tried to get her to join me & my daughter.

I was up with my mom all night. She was peaceful. We were alone. My daughter had come up from NYC & slept in the adjacent room. I gave Luella reiki. I rubbed her feet & told her I loved her. I also played your CD. It was such a comfort for me to have your music that night.

It was almost like my mantra. I just played it over & over- it kept me company.

Thank you Kathy. Please pass on my feelings of gratitude to the other members of the group. And, if you want any other feedback, please let me know.

Happy new year-

With love, Nancy

I sat in front of the wood stove one cold November morning and spread before me thirteen years of patient information intake sheets, reports and journals. I searched for old contact numbers and emails of daughters and sons and husbands and wives. Friends and partners. Names, faces and songs filled my head. There were so many here I wanted to include. Diane, joyful in her wheelchair where she lived simply in a log cabin in the woods with her devoted husband. Nancy and Bill, with his stories between songs. We were church for them when they could no longer go out. Dorrit and her birds, the way they filled the trees in September after we sang for her and circled in her yard. Every species of bird that had come to her feeders over the years, where she lived in her white farm house on the hill, had come to see her off. They gathered in the branches of the old maple over us. Birdsong filled the sky while we sang below, our feet on the earth that Dorrit was leaving, her two daughters and her son in circle with us. We all looked up. No one questioned why these birds had gathered in Dorrit's yard as she rested on her death bed, preparing to depart the world. We sang, *"Some bright morning when this life is over, I'll fly away. Like a bird from these prison walls I'll fly. I'll fly away"*

There have been many people whose generous gift of receptivity and invitation has shaped us and taught us over the years. I wanted to honor each one, to bow down and say thank you. As the responses started to flow back to me, I felt the effects of our practice. I felt the way sound waves keep moving out and out into the wider world.

Last fall, I attended a conference in Maine, a state-wide gathering of hospice choirs. Songs were sung. Food, beauty and stories were shared. The setting was gorgeous, in the town of Hallowell. This was the town our name came from—from the song written by Stephen Spitzer for his dear friend from Hallowell, after she died of a bee sting. His poetry spoke to the essence of our then-forming choir and we found our name, with Stephen's blessing.

Hallowell

I thought when someone died, the spirit flew over furthest field.
Now I see death will leave behind, a scrap of light, a broken smile,
the remnants by which I might be healed.

The dead lift me up in brightest sky.
The clouds below me race.
The dead lift me up.
I see them, see them,
face to face.

Held high by these strong hands,
breathing the wind I am born again.
The mountain flowers the desert sands,
surround me now, comfort me now.
In death or dreaming I find my kin.

Our voices shake in song
for memory we have long endured
Though this begins to make us strong
The combing through of shreds of love,
It is through living that we are cured.

I stood at the podium and looked out over a sea of shining faces in Hallowell, Maine. I spoke about gratitude and practice. I spoke about what it means to approach a bedside with reverence. And I wondered at mystery. We can never know who will respond to our call.

The chickadees stopped me in my tracks this morning. They offered me a moment of grateful reflection for all that changes. With that blessing of song, I come here to write these final pages. I am not alone, though I am on top of this wild winter frozen hill, in a quiet house. Yet I feel the presence of all of those who have died, who invited us over the years to surround their bedside and sing as they left this earth. To each of them, and to their generous families, I offer these pages with gratitude.

PART SIX

basic guidelines for quick and easy reference as used in workshops

Photo: John Nopper

SEVENTEEN

Basic Guidelines
The Practice Of Bedside Singing for the Dying
modeled after Hallowell

PREPARING FOR A SING

SELF PREPARATION

Each time you are invited to a bedside as a singer to be part of a small group, you are responsible for self-preparation. This is an individual preparation, based on your own spiritual practices/ beliefs or ways you quiet yourself within. It is best to arrive at a sing in a calm and open state of mind with little else distracting you. Having the clear intention to be in the room where someone is dying is a way to give and receive energetically with little interference.

First ask yourself if you are emotionally available for this sing. If you are feeling vulnerable or unstable or simply weary that day, saying no is a grace for everyone, most of all yourself.

If you do feel open to going to a sing, here are some preparation suggestions:

Breathe. Take long, deep, calming breaths to center yourself. Do this in your car on the way, walking down a hallway, in the elevator, on the path leading to the front door, or even standing in the doorway to the bedroom.

Meditate or Pray. If you have time to sit in quiet and center yourself and calm your mind and body before leaving for the sing, do so.

Take a meditative walk—even 5 minutes calms the nervous system and clears the head.

Ask for "guidance", whatever that means to you

Set an intention. You can do this by saying a simple phrase, either out loud or to yourself, such as;

"May I be of service"

"May I be clear of judgment"

"May I be quiet in my inner world so I can respond well and be present"

"May I be Present"

or anything that simply reminds you to let go of anxieties or thoughts or outside stimulations that might keep you from being clear, open and fully present.

The goal of self-preparation is to quiet your energy as much as possible. Assume that what each of us brings into the space is perceived or felt by those we are serving. As a person is dying, their perception may be greater than we realize so that our thoughts, emotions, attitudes, judgments and beliefs may be felt. If we try to enter the space of dying with love in our hearts, and with our highest selves present, we all—person dying, family or visitors and singers—benefit and receive the gifts of the sing.

GROUP PREPARATION

Many of the same guidelines apply to the group as a whole.
The group should always meet ahead of time, even if this takes place for just a few minutes in a driveway or yard, parking lot or lobby.

Your group leader should give you as much information as possible so you all know something about what to expect in the sense of:
—who is in the room
—what state the dying person is in
—who this person is
—song you might start with
—any information that might give you some confidence and grounding and allow you to be comfortable and present

If there is time, the group leader should sing one song with the group to connect and quiet you all together. Humming is good too.

ENTERING THE SPACE/INSIDE THE ROOM

Now that you have quieted yourself individually and as a group, you are ready to make yourselves as "small" as possible as you enter someone's home or room.

—Humming your way into a sing can be a lovely way to transition into the room without disruption

—There is no need to introduce anyone or make conversation, you are simply here to anoint this person with song. When a family is helping a loved one to die peacefully, the last thing they have energy for is social contact and new connections.

—Be aware of your breath

—Feel your feet on the ground

—Relax

—Open your heart, your eyes, your senses to what is before you

—Be aware of your emotions—allow them, welcome them and know when they are appropriate

—Stay quiet

—Sing towards the patient energetically

—Stay present—when you feel yourself checking out or feeling uncomfortable, return to breath, to song, and notice where you are. Bring yourself back again and again to the here and now. This moment is exquisite. Don't miss it.

—There should be one person who is the connect-person who talks to the family and to the patient.

—Singers should always follow the guidance of the leader.

—Only the leader chooses songs as the sing unfolds

—Leader decides when it's time to leave

—Leave as seamlessly as possible. Move slowly. Hum your way out if your leader decides this. The intention is to leave the energy you just helped to create without disruption, so the family can stay close and quiet and continue to receive the benefits of the sing after you leave.

—Stay quiet as you leave the room/house/hallway

CLOSING CIRCLE

Find a place to form a circle with your group after the sing. The place you choose to circle should offer the family privacy and not disrupt them. Be aware of your proximity to the house or the room.

This is a time to acknowledge what you have just shared and to help to integrate the experience before you leave each other.

What happens in a closing circle? This is a time to create whatever feels right as a way to bring closure to your sing. Some suggestions:

—share/process if the sing was especially intense or emotional, go around the circle and speak if you are moved to.

—sing or hum another quiet song to bring you back to balance

—breathe together with intention

—someone can offer a short spoken meditation or prayer

—share silence

Be sure to know that you can continue to process a sing afterward and that sometimes you may seek extra support through your leaders, fellow singers or resources through your local hospice. It is your responsibility to take care of yourself in this way.

DIFFERENT SITUATIONS

You will be invited to sing for many different types of situations. We like to think of this as a spectrum starting with spirited social-type of visits and continuing to the last hours of life when the sing is a way of keeping vigil, anointing and softening the energy in the room. It is then a form of prayer. You will experience everything in-between and respond accordingly, always keeping the basic guidelines in mind. Even at a "social" sing when the patient is fully alive and very responsive, a whole group of people relating and conversing can be overwhelming and exhausting. Always take cues from your leader and the family and don't assume you are there to be social.

EMOTIONS

What can you expect to feel at a sing?

Each sing will be a different experience for you. Sometimes you may feel a deep connection with a patient and/or family and be moved to tears by their story. Sometimes, the tears come because something about this particular sing resonates with you person-ally and triggers some old unresolved grief. Our emotions are a lovely expression of our inner lives, our life stories and experi-ences. They are the voice of the heart. There is no shame in feeling deeply. You can check in by asking yourself this question: Am I feeling this way because of what I'm witnessing or is this something in me personally that needs tending to? Sometimes both things are true.

Some guidelines for emotions:

Don't be afraid to feel emotional during a sing. This is emotional work. You can expect to feel deeply moved at times and even to cry. Learn to use it in your singing.

If you are feeling especially emotional, so much so that it is affecting the energy of the sing, you are welcome to remove yourself quietly from the room and wait for your group to help you to process.

Ask yourself—is this my grief or am I moved by the grief/love I see before me? This sing is not a time for you to be grieving yourself—it is someone else's story you are witnessing. However, our own stories follow us around and live within our psyches. Grief does not go away. Rather our grief becomes part of our experience of being human. You may revisit some tender places inside of yourself during or after a sing. Welcome this and use it as an opportunity to sit with it, tend it and then let it go. Again, seek more support from leaders or hospice counselors if needed. And never be a harsh judge if you are feeling full of emotion or if you have to leave a sing. Remember, it is the voice of your own heart singing. Your own wisdom will lead you in knowing how to use the grief in the best way possible.

THE PRACTICE

Think of being part of a hospice choir as a practice in your life. You will have opportunity after opportunity to practice:
 —quieting of mind, body and spirit
 —being fully present
 —letting go of ego/judgment of self and others
 —letting go of expectations—"don't know mind" or "beginner's mind" is best each time

—serving—giving and receiving

—listening with your heart

—responding from a place of clarity and truth

—accepting "what is"

—gratitude

—singing with spirit

—living fully

—not needing to change or fix what doesn't need to be changed or fixed.

As I once heard from yoga teacher Paul Spector: This is a practice of "radical noninterference with what is". If that's all you remember— you will be gifted with grace.

ACKNOWLEDGMENTS

Trying to express gratitude for the birth of this book is like trying to find the beginning and ending of a circle. Where to begin? Without those people who have died before us and invited us to be singers around them as they died, there would be no book. Without the many singers who have been part of Hallowell for the past thirteen years, there would be no music. Without the wonderful directors and teachers of our songs, there would be none for us to sing. Without the constant support of Brattleboro Area Hospice we would be disconnected from the community we serve. And without the loving support of my family and community of close friends, I would not be the resource I am to make this possible. We are all part of the circle.

Thank you to all of the families who gave permission to use these stories, all true, about our visits with their dying beloveds. I am eternally grateful that we were invited into your lives during a time of raw emotion and intimacy. For the families I could not contact, I am equally grateful and have changed names, locations and details to preserve your privacy. I am especially grateful to: Fred, Lauren and Katharine Breunig, David Baker, Carol Whitaker, Beth Smallheer, Eve Ness, Jim Mullen and family, Oona Madden and family, Kate Dodge, Mark Schlefer, Alice Gauche and Trish, Victor and Julie

Good, Martha, Leo and Ann, Nancy Conklin-Stone, Kate Conklin, Jay Conklin, MaryLu Mills, Christine Mills, Beverly and Steve Green, Sarah Pierce and Tony, Genie Shields, Chris Triebert, Carol Maniscalchi, Carol Perry, Mary Rosen, Edie Mas.

To Rod MacIver for the beautiful artwork that graces the front cover and your generosity in sharing it.

To John Nopper for his expression of and his appreciation for Hallowell through the lens of his camera.

Thank you to Linda Worster for permission to use lyrics to her song "Spirit Friend". And to Stephen Spitzer for permission to use lyrics to his song "Hallowell".

For your voices in praise and support: Bernice Mennis, Jan Frazier, Camilla Rockwell and Ira Byock, MD. Thank you for reading and responding with such care.

For Camilla Rockwell whose 2006 production of the film *Holding Our Own: Embracing the End of Life*, which features Hallowell, inspired the growth and movement of bedside singing for the dying across the country.

To those who helped me shape this project. Bernice Mennis for your compassionate, kind and deep intelligence. Thank you for reading/editing/shaping and cheering me on. You are a true teacher of writing, ideas and most of all spirit.

To Maureen Moore at Booksmyth Press for endless hours of your time, for your creative eye and especially for your great well of patience and quick responses to my constant demands.

To the many friends who helped this project along through continued conversation, encouragement and support, you are all part of this circle. Wendy, David, Juliette, Maggie C, Alice F, all of my extended Red Clover family, soul collage group, poetry group, writing group, meditation group, and too many to remember or list, but trust you are here.

Gratitude and praise for Lisa Sparrow who influenced Hallowell's beginning and continues to be part of the circle of song and spirit that serve our community.

Thank you to my manuscript writing group who read through these pages as they developed over a year. Each of you helped to shape this guidebook. Ceacy Henderson, Dianne Hunter, Nancy Smith, Penfield Chester, Liz Bedell, and Rebecca Southwick. A special thank you to Patricia Lee Lewis who created the Manuscript Series at Patchwork Farm and held a beautiful space for us to work within. Another circle.

I want to express enormous gratitude to Brattleboro Area Hospice (BAH). In 2002, I took the hospice volunteer training taught by Noree Ennis and the first seeds for Hallowell were planted. Thank you Noree for your loving kindness, your vision and your encouragement to create Hallowell and bring music to any of our clients who desired the gift of song at the end of life. To all of the staff at BAH who continue to support our practice in every possible way; by offering our service of singing to clients, inviting us to sing at hospice related events, and making us part of the exceptional and soulful team of caring individuals that make up BAH. Susan Parris, Connie Baxter, Bettina Berg, Elizabeth Pittman, Cheryl Richards, Joanna Rueter, Cicely Carroll, Joyce Drew, Andrea Livermore, and especially to Ryan Murphy and Patty Dunn, Hospice Care Coordinators, who work so closely with the families we are asked to sing for.

To all of the growing hospice choirs. Thank you for your support and commitment over the years.

Thank you to each and every Hallowell singer who has dedicated time and heart to this practice. Some have come and gone over the years, others have remained members from the start. You are all part of this story. Every time you say yes and show up at a sing, I am filled with the gratitude I tried to express in these pages. These are the singers who make up Hallowell in 2016 but to those of you who have moved on, you are here as well. Mary Alice Amidon, Helen Anglos, Susan Barduhn, Margaret Dale Barrand, Tony Barrand, Susan Bell, Fred Breunig, Larry Crockett, Ellen Crockett, Robin Davis, Jamie Eckley, Hans Estrin, Calvin Farwell, Leslie Goldman, Tom Goldschmid, Eliza Greenhoe, Mark Grieco, Annie Guion, Amy Harlow, Tom Jamison, Valerie Kosednar, Bonnie Kraft, Beth Lukin, Cathy MacDonald, Manny Mansbach, Cathy Martin, Mike Mayer, Kathy Michel, Jonathan Morse, Patrice Murray, Karolina Oleksiw, Susan Owings, Susie Peters, Julie Peterson, Bob Rueter, Joan Shimer, Walter Slowinski, Beth Spicer, Terry Sylvester, Burt Tepfer, Harriet Tepfer, Cindy Tolman, Gill Truslow, and Connie Woodberry.

To Mary Cay Brass and Peter Amidon, beloved friends and extraordinary music directors/teachers for Hallowell. Your gifts and talents have been generously shared to grow this practice. You continue to give your time, your expertise and your hearts to Hallowell and to the practice of bedside singing. Teaching beside you two at workshops has been a natural and formidable experience. This practice, our music and this book would not exist without your part in all of it. Thank you with all my heart.

To Erik, father of my children, for many years of support that helped me shape the world of Hallowell in the early days.

To my daughter Melissa, for your attentive read-through when you had so much else calling your time and attention, for your hawk's eye for detail, but most of all and simply for being my most treasured and beloved daughter. You fill my life because you are in the world.

To my son Jason. Your gentle nature and soulful heart continue to teach me how to bring grace to everything I do.

My children are with me at every bedside, reminding me of what love feels like. When I am witness to another family's grief and love, I understand with compassion because of my love for my own children. This love, of course, extends to Fin, my grandson who came into the world and cracked open a fifth chamber of my heart reserved for grandmothers. Thank you Fin, for the light you bring to my life. This book was born from that light.

And to Tom, my Anam Cara, my beloved life partner. You are beside me at the bedside as we sing for the dying. You are beside me in our gardens, at our kitchen table, in our warm bed, our loving home and most of all, you live in every room of my heart. What would I do without you?

May the Circle Be Unbroken

To order Hallowell CDs "Angels Hovering Round" and "Love Call Me Home" go to: www.hallowell-singers.org.
For more hospice related music visit these sites:
www.amidonmusic.com
https://marycaybrass.com/